Enduring Work

Enduring Work

Experiences with Canada's Temporary Foreign Worker Program

Catherine E. Connelly

McGill-Queen's University Press
Montreal & Kingston • London • Chicago

ISBN 978-0-2280-1667-0 (cloth)
ISBN 978-0-2280-1668-7 (paper)
ISBN 978-0-2280-1799-8 (ePDF)
ISBN 978-0-2280-1800-1 (ePUB)

Legal deposit second quarter 2023
Bibliothèque nationale du Québec

Printed in Canada on acid-free paper that is 100% ancient forest free
(100% post-consumer recycled), processed chlorine free

This book has been published with the help of a grant from the Canadian Federation
for the Humanities and Social Sciences, through the Awards to Scholarly Publications
Program, using funds provided by the Social Sciences and Humanities Research
Council of Canada.

Funded by the   Financé par le
Government   gouvernement
of Canada   du Canada

Canada Council   Conseil des arts
for the Arts   du Canada

We acknowledge the support of the Canada Council for the Arts.

Nous remercions le Conseil des arts du Canada de son soutien.

Library and Archives Canada Cataloguing in Publication

Title: Enduring work : experiences with Canada's Temporary Foreign Worker Program /
    Catherine E. Connelly.

Names: Connelly, Catherine E., author.

Description: Includes bibliographical references and index.

Identifiers: Canadiana (print) 20220480923 | Canadiana (ebook) 20220480966 |
    ISBN 9780228016687 (paper) | ISBN 9780228016670 (cloth) | ISBN 9780228018001
    (ePUB) | ISBN 9780228017998 (ePDF)

Subjects: LCSH: Temporary Foreign Workers Program (Canada) | LCSH: Foreign
    workers – Government policy – Canada. | LCSH: Foreign workers – Canada –
    Social conditions. | LCSH: Organizational behavior – Canada. | LCSH: Personnel
    management – Canada.

Classification: LCC HD8108.5 .c66 2023 | DDC 331.6/20971 – dc23

This book was designed and typeset by Peggy & Co. Design in 10.5/13 Sabon.

Contents

Tables

Acknowledgments

I am grateful for the financial support for this research from the Social Sciences and Humanities Research Council, the Canada Research Chairs Program, and the DeGroote School of Business at McMaster University. Scholarly research is time- and resource-intensive, and the funding that I received enabled me to collect and analyze the data that forms the basis of this book.

I am also so thankful for the people who took time from their days off to talk to me so candidly about their experiences with the Canadian Temporary Foreign Worker program. Their stories were always informative and sometimes emotional, and some of their stories continue to haunt me.

For scholars who also have teaching and service responsibilities, paid research assistance is crucially important. I was extraordinarily fortunate to have the support of Anne St-Amand, my research coordinator. Her assistance was invaluable, because of her extraordinary attention to detail, and she helped to track down the answers to so many of my questions, while handling so many complex logistical issues. Anne recruited and screened the participants, scheduled our interviews, and ensured that the participants were paid. She also helped with the interviews and translations, the transcriptions, and tracking down supplemental information. Anne's help was essential during my unexpected medical leave and gradual return to work. I am also grateful for the assistance of Ani Chénier, who filled in for Anne during her leave.

I am also very appreciative of the assistance of Colette Nyirakamana, Riva Gewarges, Angela Licata, and Alexandra Lefcoe, who conducted some of the interviews for this project. Antoinette Forcione, Sue Hamilton, Jeneta Rubaranjan, Monika Pobiedzinski, Thusitha Suriyakumar, Adam Buffett, and Angela Licata transcribed the interviews. I am grateful for the help of Daniela Dobrota, an immigration lawyer, who verified the accuracy of the definitions of the various streams of the TFW program.

I also appreciate the help of Dan Kelly, from the Canadian Federation of Independent Businesses (CFIB), who helped put me in touch with employers who had experience using the TFW program.

This book has been on my mind for years, and I am fortunate to have been able to discuss this project over the years with Silvia Bonaccio, Michelle Buckley, Lance Ferris, Judy Fudge, Rick Hackett, Benson Honig, Sandy Hershcovis, John Medcof, Erin Reid, Trish Ruebottom, Aaron Schat, Andrew Stevens, Danielle van Jaarsveld, and many other colleagues. I am also grateful to the scholars in the audience at the Canadian Industrial Relations Association conference where I presented some of my findings.

Many thanks to Jonathan Crago and Jacqueline Mason, who were so enthusiastic about the project from the beginning, and to Emily Andrew who helped me to navigate the review process. I also appreciate the help of Lisa Aitken, Joanne Pisano, and Filomena Falocco, who helped to publish the book. I am also very grateful to the two anonymous reviewers, who read the manuscript so carefully and who had so many helpful suggestions.

I also appreciate the help of Beth McAuley and Gillian Scobie, who helped me edit my prose so that it was more accessible to both a specialist and lay audience, as well as Michel Pharand, who created a thorough and nuanced index. All errors are, of course, my own.

A special thanks to Jane Nicholas, Judith Leggett, and Monica Flegel, who first suggested that I write this book and then answered so many questions and provided so much encouragement.

Most important has been the support and encouragement of Adam Van Tuyl and Iris Connelly-Van Tuyl. I love them both dearly.

Enduring Work

was somewhat skeptical about whether they had sufficiently explored other recruitment options. Many of these managers were aware of the mistreatment that their own TFWs had experienced (e.g., from their previous employers) and were dismayed that this had happened to someone they liked and respected. They were generally very pleased with the calibre of workers they had hired, and usually described them as being hard-working and family-oriented. However, the managers also expressed significant concerns with the way in which the TFW program was being run; they often found the program to be cumbersome, expensive, and unresponsive to the needs of employers.

Enduring Work

As flawed as the TFW program is, it is likely to endure in some form because of the continued needs (and lobbying efforts) of Canadian businesses that depend on it. The purpose of this book is twofold: first, to bring new evidence into the debates about this program. Rather than focusing primarily on the experiences of a single type of TFW (e.g., in-home caregivers) or workers from a single region or occupation who are working in a specific region of Canada, I take a wider view and examine a broader cross-section of workers that includes all four categories of TFWs: the in-home caregivers, the seasonal agricultural workers, and the high-wage and low-wage workers. By doing so, I am able to compare their experiences and offer some insights into the unique risk factors for each stream of the TFW program as well as for TFWs in general. I also examine the experiences of a wide cross-section of employers who hire TFWs, noting that, as with the TFWs, this is not a homogenous group. This broader approach allows me to distinguish some underlying mindsets that may be associated with employers' use or misuse of the TFW program.

Second, this book incorporates an organizational behaviour and human resources management perspective that has largely been absent from discussions about the Canadian TFW program. In so doing, I complement the research that has been conducted in other fields. Organizational behaviour is the study of individuals and groups within an organizational context, focusing on attributes, processes, behaviours, and outcomes such as performance and well-being.[1] Human resources management focuses on organizations' practices regarding recruitment and selection, compensation and benefits, occupational health and safety management, as well as performance management.[2] These perspectives are useful for understanding both employees' and employers' experiences with the TFW program, especially organizations' use of third parties (e.g., employment agencies and immigration consultants) and strategic HR planning (e.g., the decision to use TFWs instead of hiring locally). Both academic disciplines offer insights into TFWs' career management strategies, such as which country they move to and how their social networks can be leveraged or are adversely affected by these moves.

Implicit in some of the public discussions about the Canadian TFW program is an assumption that there is a trade-off between TFWs' poor experiences with the program and the benefits that accrue to employers that use it. In this book, I argue that TFWs' experiences are worse than is commonly acknowledged, and that employers are not benefiting as much as one might think.

An Overview of the Canadian TFW Program

The Temporary Foreign Worker program in Canada has been a source of much interest for Canadians. Part of the public interest in this long-standing government initiative stems from its sheer size; in 2018, a total of 78,788 new TFW program permits were approved,[3] not accounting for the TFWs already in Canada on multi-year work permits. There has also been considerable media attention about the program over the past several years. Many Canadians will remember the waitresses in Saskatchewan in 2014 who were fired from their long-held jobs because their employer instead honoured its contracts with the TFWs who had been hired a few months before.[4] More recently, Canadians learned of the appalling living conditions experienced by TFWs working on mushroom farms in Ontario[5] and the unsafe working conditions experienced by truck drivers in British Columbia.[6]

However, most foreign workers in Canada are *not* TFWs. The Canadian government issues several types of work permits to people from other countries, and most of these work permits are issued through the International Mobility Program (IMP), not the TFW program. From the employers' perspective, the most important difference between the two programs is that the IMP does not require a Labour Market Impact Assessment (LMIA). The LMIA is only required for the TFW program. Its primary purpose is to demonstrate that no qualified Canadians are available to do the job in question. Furthermore, the IMP is administered by Immigration Canada, whereas the TFW program is administered by both Immigration, Refugees and Citizenship Canada

Table 0.1 Comparing the Canadian International Mobility Program and the Temporary Foreign Worker Program

	International Mobility Program (IMP)	Temporary Foreign Worker (TFW) Program
Requires a Labour Market Impact Assessment (LMIA)	✗	✓
Administered by	Immigration, Refugees and Citizenship Canada (IRCC)	Immigration, Refugees and Citizenship Canada (IRCC) and Employment and Social Development Canada (ESDC)
Covers refugee claimants, spouses of high-wage TFWs, students, and people who have applied for permanent residency	✓	✗
Covers skilled workers from countries with whom Canada has a free-trade agreement	✓	✗

(IRCC) and Employment and Social Development Canada (ESDC). The IMP covers many different types of workers, including refugee claimants, spouses of high-wage TFWs, students, and people who have applied for permanent residency. It also covers *skilled* (but not unskilled) workers from countries with whom Canada has a free-trade agreement such as the North American Free Trade Agreement (i.e., the United States and Mexico), the Comprehensive and Economic Trade Agreement (i.e., twenty-eight countries, including Germany, France, Italy), the Comprehensive and Progressive Agreement for Trans-Pacific Partnership (e.g., seven countries, including Australia, Japan, Singapore) as well as several agreements covering other exceptions (e.g., some airline personnel). In this book, I focus only on the workers who are covered under the TFW program, not the IMP.

The TFWs in Canada are notably different from the IMP workers in that TFWs have closed work permits; this means that they must remain with the employer who hires them for the duration of their stay in Canada. If TFWs quit or are fired, they must return to their country of origin or find a new employer that happens to have a job vacancy and an LMIA. Their original employer can then apply to hire a replacement TFW.

The TFW program comprises several occupational streams, each with important differences. In this book, I focus on four of these: the Seasonal Agricultural Worker Program (SAWP); the in-home caregiver stream (before 2019 known as the live-in caregiver stream); the low-wage TFW stream (before 2019 known as the lower-skill stream); and the high-wage TFW stream (before 2019 known as the higher-skill stream). I provide more detail about the current versions of these streams below.

Although the TFW program currently encompasses a broad variety of industries and occupations, this was not always the case. Initially, the number of foreign workers entering Canada on a temporary basis was relatively small. The first TFWs arrived in Canada from Jamaica in 1966 to work seasonally in agriculture, and in 1967 the program was expanded to include both Barbados and Trinidad and Tobago.[7] Gradually, the program expanded; in 1973, it began including workers from Mexico, and in 1976 the program grew again to include workers from Eastern Caribbean countries.[8] In 1981 and 1984, there was significant political pressure to limit the number of agricultural workers entering Canada as part of the TFW program, but farming associations (e.g., the Canadian Horticultural Council) applied enough pressure to allow the program to continue to grow.[9] A few years later, in 1987, the administration of the SAWP was privatized. Since then, it has remained under the control of the Foreign Agricultural Resource Management Services (i.e., FARMS), a non-profit organization that facilitates the hiring process for workers in the SAWP. At the same time, the annual quotas on the number of workers were lifted – thereby signalling the further expansion of the TFW program.

Meanwhile, starting in 1955, a growing number of workers had been entering Canada to be employed as in-home caregivers or "domestic" workers after the federal government introduced an early version of the in-home caregiver program known as the West Indian Domestic Scheme.[10] This program differed from the agricultural TFW programs in that it enabled workers to immigrate rather than simply providing them with temporary status. However, this program ended in 1968 and was replaced with a points-based system. In 1981, under the Foreign Domestic Movement Program, foreign "domestic" workers who had lived in Canada for two years were allowed to apply for landed immigrant status. However, to be successful, these workers needed to provide evidence of occupational upgrading, i.e., doing volunteer work to demonstrate "social adaptation" to the community and public life in Canada; and "financial security," i.e., personal savings. These criteria were widely criticized because they were not applied to other occupations that were male-dominated.[11] The 1992 Live-In Caregiver Program shifted this role by professionalizing it; "domestic workers" were now referred to as caregivers, and new education and work experience requirements were introduced.[12]

A precursor of the high-wage and low-wage TFW programs began in 1973 when the Non-Immigrant Employment Authorization Program (NIEAP) was introduced, allowing interested workers to apply for closed work permits from outside Canada. The permits tied workers to a single employer and required them to receive written permission from immigration officials to alter their conditions of work or to change employers.[13] Up until 2002, more than half of temporary foreign workers were considered to be highly skilled, but that changed with the introduction of the Low-Skill Pilot Project, which was expanded in 2006.[14] These initiatives facilitated the hiring of TFWs for low-skill occupations that were deemed to be "under pressure," (i.e., high demand for and low supply of workers) and reduced employers' obligation to demonstrate that a qualified Canadian could not be hired. Between 2007 and 2010, the administrative requirements for thirty-three skilled and low-skilled occupations were relaxed in British Columbia and Alberta under the Expedited Labour Market Opinion (E-LMO) program.[15] In 2012, this was expanded to all provinces for managers and skilled occupations, under the Accelerated Labour Market Opinion (A-LMO).[16] However, in 2013 these initiatives were suspended and later eliminated.[17]

We see from the way in which the various streams of the TFW program have unfolded that there is a continual tension between employer requests to admit more workers and calls to restrict or curtail worker access to the program. Although the four streams of the TFW program all have closed work permits, there are key differences between the features of these streams and the workers who typically access them. The typical TFW may be an agricultural worker from Mexico or an in-home caregiver from the Philippines, but the diversity of the Canadian TFW program – in terms of workers' occupations, industries, and nationalities – is sometimes overlooked. It would thus be instructive to consider the breadth of these workers' experiences.

Before I describe the current TFW program streams in more detail, it is important to note that the TFW program has changed continuously since its inception, and is likely to continue to change. My research was conducted between 2014 and 2019, so I describe the key elements of the relevant streams as they existed during this period.

Seasonal Agricultural Worker Program (SAWP)

The Seasonal Agricultural Worker Program is the largest TFW stream in Canada (45,105 permits approved in 2017).[18] TFWs in the SAWP program can only work within the boundaries of a farm, nursery, or greenhouse, and they must either (a) operate farm equipment; (b) be involved with the boarding, care, breeding, sanitation, or other handling of farm animals (other than fish) for the purpose of obtaining raw animal products for market; (c) be involved in collecting, handling, and assessing these animal products; or (d) be involved in planting, caring for, harvesting, or preparing crops, trees, sod, or other plants for market; in addition, (e) the job title/position has to correspond to specific National Occupation Classification (NOC) codes that are defined by the Government of Canada. For example, farm labourers might pick fruit or vegetables or they might take care of beef cattle.

This program has shifted somewhat over the years; today, there are bilateral agreements with Mexico[19] and with eleven Caribbean countries (Anguilla, Antigua and Barbuda, Barbados, Dominica, Grenada, Jamaica, Montserrat, St Kitts-Nevis, St Lucia, St Vincent and the Grenadines, and Trinidad and Tobago),[20] with most workers coming from Mexico and Jamaica. It is important to distinguish the SAWP from the agricultural TFW program stream, which only applies to workers in the agricultural sector who do not hail from one of these twelve countries.

In 2019, workers who were part of the SAWP program could only work for a single employer at a time. It is possible for employers to transfer workers from one farm to another as long as the employer has the worker's consent, prior written approval from the relevant foreign government representative in Canada, and prior written approval from ESDC. However, employers cannot informally share workers with other farms, or transfer them to other farms without prior approval; doing so is punishable by a fine of up to $50,000 and imprisonment.[21] Contracts are in place to provide oversight. Each contract must span a maximum of eight months and the worker must return to their country of origin after the contract expires, although workers frequently return to the same employer for several years in a row. The contract must be signed by the employer, the employee, and the liaison officer for the foreign government, and it must be provided to the employee in French or English, and Spanish.

To access the SAWP, prospective employers do not need to *pay* for a Labour Market Impact Assessment (unlike the other streams in the TFW program). However, they must still complete the relevant LMIA paperwork, demonstrate that they have not been able to recruit Canadian workers, and provide proof of business legitimacy. In practice, this means that employers must advertise their positions widely (e.g., on employment websites, such as the national Job Bank) for a minimum of fourteen calendar days within a three-month period before they apply to the government to hire a TFW. This process has been criticized because there is often a mismatch between when the positions are advertised, when they begin, and when workers would be available. As described in more detail in chapter 5, companies sometimes post a job far in advance of when the position would begin. Because most Canadian job seekers are looking for jobs that start immediately, they are unlikely to apply for these jobs. The company is then able to demonstrate that it cannot find Canadians to do the necessary work – thus establishing a need to hire TFWs. This process goes against the spirit of the TFW guidelines.

Employers must provide SAWP workers with return transportation from their place of residence to the worksite in Canada (e.g., airfare), although a portion of these costs can be recovered through payroll deductions (except in British Columbia). They must also provide daily transportation to the work site, as well as "adequate, suitable and affordable housing," which is subject to inspection.[22] These employment benefits are offered for practical reasons (e.g., the cost of flying to Canada could be prohibitive for many applicants; providing housing may be cheaper and more convenient than arranging transportation to a rural location), but for both the Canadian and the partner government it also achieves the goal of ensuring that the workers return to their country of origin at the end of their contracts.

Because these workers are employed in Canada, their working conditions are governed by provincial health and safety acts. In every province, employers must ensure that all TFWs are covered by an appropriate (provincial or equivalent) workplace safety insurance provider, and, where applicable, that all employees on the worksite are covered by the same provider. Employers must take all possible and reasonable precautions to protect the health and safety of all their workers; ensure that equipment, materials, and protective equipment are maintained and in good condition; provide information, instruction, and supervision to protect workers; and cooperate with health and safety representatives and joint health and safety committees. All employees have the right to refuse unsafe work, know the hazards of their workplace, and participate in decisions that could affect their safety.[23] For example, employers using pesticides or other hazardous chemicals must notify workers of these hazards, provide free protective equipment, and provide appropriate training on how to use the pesticides and chemicals safely. All TFWs must be paid the same wages and benefits, including overtime pay, as those paid to Canadian employees working in the same occupation.[24]

To seek employment through this program, prospective workers register with their own (foreign) government, and pay a fee. The foreign government selects individuals who they believe will be good workers (e.g., experienced in farming, at least eighteen years old);[25] and who will return home after the end of the contract (e.g., those already married, with children or other dependents); and they ensure that the paperwork is in order. The worker referral process is managed by the foreign governments. Once a worker has been approved, their name goes onto a list, and the farms in Canada can choose them specifically or simply request any approved worker from a particular country.

Farms typically resubmit the names of the workers they have hired previously (assuming they performed well and got along well with other employees) as well as those recommended by current or former employees. SAWP employees pay their work permit fees directly to Immigration, Refugees and Citizenship Canada (IRCC).

The SAWP has received considerable criticism because of workers' living and working conditions. Nor do these workers have a path to permanent residency and subsequent Canadian citizenship, although they make contributions to the Canadian Pension Plan and pay federal and provincial taxes on their wages. Workers who are part of the SAWP program are also discouraged from bringing their families with them.[26]

In-Home Caregiver (Live-in Caregiver) Stream

In 2019, the live-in caregiver program (which had 7,787 permits approved in 2016)[27] was renamed the in-home caregiver stream. These initiatives were designed to enable Canadian families to hire workers to provide full-time in-home care for children and relatives with high medical needs (e.g., seniors, people with disabilities or illnesses). Most caregivers employed through both streams are female and come to Canada from the Philippines.

Employers must abide by certain requirements. In-home caregivers must work in their employer's home, but, as of 2014, they cannot be required to live there, though employers could require this as a condition of employment. As of 2019, employers could no longer require this. In practice, however, most in-home caregivers do live in their employer's home, either for financial reasons or because of implicit pressure to do so. If they are providing accommodation, the worker must have their own separate furnished room in the employer's house with a lock and safety bolt on the inside of the door.[28] This bedroom must meet certain requirements (e.g., it must have a window) and the caregiver cannot be charged for room and board. In-home caregivers are also generally entitled to receive return transportation to the work location in Canada from their country of origin. The employer cannot recover this cost from the employee.[29] No contract can be longer than twenty-four months. Caregivers are legally entitled to the same labour standards as workers who are Canadian or permanent residents (e.g., being paid minimum wage or prevailing median wages). Their contracts stipulate that they should receive set working hours with breaks, they are entitled to overtime if they work more than forty-four hours per week, and this overtime cannot be calculated on the basis of the average number of hours worked in a pay period. Employers cannot require in-home caregivers to do tasks unrelated to the job for which they received the LMIA; for example, caregivers cannot be required to do housework, remove snow, or do yardwork.[30]

In contrast to agricultural workers, in-home caregivers have a clear path to permanent residency and Canadian citizenship. Before applying to work in Canada, they need one year of full-time work experience as an in-home childcare or support worker and must meet minimum language and education requirements. Once they have worked in Canada for twenty-four months of full-time employment as an in-home caregiver during a thirty-six month period, they are able to apply for permanent residency. To access the program, potential caregivers need to pay relevant fees to their home (non-Canadian) government and provide documentation to prove that they meet the educational requirements of the position to which they are applying (i.e., the equivalent of one year of post-secondary education in Canada). Many in-home caregivers find work through word of mouth with friends and relatives who are already living in Canada. However, many agencies recruit in-home caregivers and typically charge fees from $500 to $1,500 per worker.

Families that wish to hire an in-home caregiver can do so by submitting an LMIA application.[31] These employers are also required to pay a non-refundable fee of $1,000 to cover the costs of the application, unless they are hiring the caregiver to take care of someone with high medical needs or their gross annual income is $150,000 or less.[32] Employers must ensure that the caregiver speaks English or French fluently enough to communicate effectively, but they cannot require that the caregiver be fluent in any other languages. As with the SAWP, employers must demonstrate that they were unable to hire a Canadian for the position and provide evidence that they advertised the position on the national Job Bank or on equivalent provincial job websites. Employers must also provide proof that a dependent is in need of care (e.g., proof of a child or senior's age, a physician's note attesting to the dependent's disability), as well as proof that they are able to pay the caregiver's wages (e.g., a copy of the Notice of Assessment from the Canada Revenue Agency).[33]

High-Wage (Higher-Skill) TFW Stream

The high-wage TFW stream replaced the higher-skill TFW stream in 2019.[34] Before 2019, a job was classified as being eligible for the higher-skill TFW program depending on the NOC code for the position. This classification took into account the knowledge, skills, education, and credentials required to do the job. Positions for higher-skill TFWs had to have a NOC code of 0 (management jobs), A (professional jobs that usually require a university degree), or B (technical jobs and skilled trades that usually require a college diploma or apprenticeship). These jobs typically required post-secondary education, and included a wide range of occupations (e.g., bakers and chefs, forepersons, accountants, videographers, and animators). Starting in 2019, the LMIA was classified as either "high-wage" or "low-wage," depending on whether the hourly wage was above or below the median provincial or territorial hourly wage (e.g., $28.85 in Alberta, $21.63 in Prince Edward Island). The NOC codes, along with data about the median wages for these NOC codes in different regions, are now used to determine the wages that must be paid to the high-wage TFW who is hired. The median wages are calculated based on the annual Statistics Canada Labour Force Survey and the data prepared by Emploi-Québec.

Prospective employers need to complete the specific LMIA application that is designated for high-wage positions, and pay a non-refundable processing fee of $1,000 for each TFW they would like to hire.[35] As part of this application, employers must:

- show that no qualified Canadian citizens or permanent residents are available for the job;
- provide specific details about how the job was advertised (e.g., the national Job Bank, Indeed: Job Search Canada, as well as other online job-search websites);
- show how many applications were received from Canadians or permanent residents;

- show how many Canadians or permanent residents were interviewed and offered the job, were hired, or declined the job;
- show how many Canadian citizens or permanent residents applied but were not interviewed or offered the position;[36]
- indicate the reasons why each Canadian or permanent resident who applied but who was deemed unsuitable did not meet the requirements of the position.[37]

The TFW needs to be paid at least the local median wage for the occupation, which is calculated based on Canadian or Quebec government data for the area. The employer does not need to pay for the accommodation or transportation costs of the high-wage TFWs. These workers frequently bring their spouses and dependent children with them to Canada, although they must obtain separate permits to work or study at a post-secondary institution. The high-wage TFW is protected by all the same employment standards legislation as Canadians, in terms of hours of work (including overtime), compensation, working conditions (including health and safety), and termination of employment.

With the exception of the simplified LMIA that is available to Quebec employers in some circumstances, the employer must also develop and explain a transition plan for how they will transition to a Canadian workforce while the high-wage TFW is working there. If the employer has hired TFWs previously, they must provide an update on how the existing transition plan is proceeding, and why another TFW is necessary.[38] The transition plan could have two general strategies. It could involve at least three distinct activities (e.g., increase wages offered, offer part-time or flexible hours, partner with unions or industry associations to identify potential candidates) to recruit, retain, and train Canadians or permanent residents. The plan could also use one additional distinct activity to recruit qualified employees from underrepresented groups (e.g., immigrants, Indigenous people, youth, people with disabilities).[39] Alternatively, the employer could plan to support a TFW's application for permanent residency.[40]

Low-Wage (Lower-Skill) Stream

The low-wage stream of the TFW program is perhaps the most controversial of the TFW programs. In 2019, it replaced the lower-skill TFW stream (which itself replaced the low-skill TFW stream that had been redesigned in 2014). The process for hiring low-wage TFWs mirrors that for the high-wage TFWs described above, except for some additional requirements and restrictions for the low-wage stream. For example, some occupations are ineligible for the low-wage TFW stream, including security guards, cashiers, janitors, and landscapers (although these occupations were eligible for the earlier lower-skill TFW program).[41]

The NOC defined which occupations were eligible for the earlier lower-skill TFW stream by coding them as level C (requires high school education and/or job-specific training) or D (requires on-the-job training). These positions typically did not require post-secondary education, but they may have required some occupation-specific training (e.g., truck drivers), and the TFW who held one of these positions may have had qualifications that exceeded the actual requirements of the position. In contrast to the lower-skill TFW stream, the new low-wage stream focuses on the wages allocated to the position rather than exclusively on the NOC code, although, as noted above, there are exceptions. A job is eligible for the low-wage TFW stream if the hourly wage is below the median provincial or territorial hourly wage, as described above.

Employers who would like to hire a low-wage TFW need to complete the Labour Market Impact Assessment Application – Low-Wage Positions form and pay a fee of $1,000 to apply to use the program.[42] In 2014, the total number of low-wage positions available to each company was capped; in 2019, the cap was set at 20 per cent of the company's workforce if the company had used the lower-skill TFW program before 20 June 2014; otherwise, the cap was set at 10 per cent of the company's workforce.[43] As of September 2019, the number of TFWs that would be nominated for a Provincial Nominee Program certificate or Certificat de sélection du Québec was taken into account when calculating the cap;[44] before 2019, this factor was not considered. Exemptions to the cap are available under special circumstances: if the business has fewer than ten employees nationally, if the position is for project-based work that will last for 120 or fewer days, or the position is in a seasonal industry and the TFW will not be needed for longer than 180 days. As with the high-wage TFW stream, the employer must demonstrate that no qualified Canadians are available to be hired and provide specific details on how the job was advertised, how many applications it received from Canadians or permanent residents, how many Canadians or permanent residents it interviewed and offered the job, were hired or declined the job, as well as how many Canadians or permanent residents applied but were not interviewed or offered the position. The employer must also explain why each Canadian or permanent resident who applied was not hired. Also, employers are not eligible to hire a low-wage TFW if they are located in an area with an unemployment rate of 6 per cent or higher.[45]

Low-wage TFWs are protected by all the same employment standards legislation that applies to Canadians: hours of work (including overtime), compensation, working conditions (including health and safety), and termination of employment.[46] Low-wage TFWs must be paid at minimum the prevailing wage for their occupation, which is the higher of either the median wage listed on the Job Bank website, or the wages paid to current employees hired for the same job and work location, with the same skills and years of experience. These wages do not include tips, overtime hours, and other bonuses or commissions. The employer must also pay for low-wage TFWs' round-trip transportation to Canada and ensure that suitable and affordable housing is available (i.e., not costing more than 30 per cent of the worker's before-tax income).[47] Technically, these workers are able to bring their spouses and dependent children with them to Canada, but the spouses and children are not eligible to work unless they obtain a separate work permit, which is difficult to obtain (unlike the spouses of high-wage TFWs, who are routinely granted work permits through a separate category in the IMP).

An Overview of This Book

This book contains six chapters. In chapter 1, "Subtle Differences in the Types of Mistreatment Endured by Different Groups of TFWs," I describe the experiences of participants in the SAWP, the in-home caregiver program, the low-wage TFW program, and the high-wage TFW program, and explain how the structures and characteristics of the different programs affect these workers' experiences. Within each stream of the TFW program, all workers are vulnerable to mistreatment, but racialized workers from the Global South are much more likely than their peers to be mistreated. Moreover, although TFWs in the high-wage program are more educated and have more social capital than participants in the other programs, my evidence suggests that these workers still endure mistreatment – especially if they are from the Global South. Their qualifications and experience make them vulnerable to employers exploiting them by requiring them to perform tasks not stipulated in their contracts; their high wages make them attractive targets for wage theft and requests for illegal employment fees; and they also endure dangerous occupational health and safety conditions.

One might assume that the use of international employment agencies and immigration consultants should make recruiting, selecting, and settling TFWs more efficient for both workers and employers. Employers must strictly adhere to government protocols, and first-time users may find them confusing. However, in chapter 2, "Enduring Problems with Agents," I use agency theory to explain why the inherent structure of the relationships between TFWs and employment agencies or immigration consultants as well as the relationships between employers and employment agencies or immigration consultants are consistently exploitative. Agents (i.e., employment agencies and immigration consultants), employers, and TFWs have fundamentally different goals: agents and employers each seek to maximize their profit whereas TFWs seek employment in Canada. Both employers and TFWs have difficulty monitoring and verifying the actions of agents, and this absence of reliable information can provide agents with the opportunity to provide suboptimal service or fraudulent activities.

Given TFWs' difficulties during their job search and while employed in Canada, they would benefit from the social support of their friends and families. Unfortunately, the way the TFW program is structured frequently increases the physical and psychological distance between TFWs and their existing social networks, making it difficult for these workers to expand their networks while in Canada. In chapter 3, "Family: Social Capital under Strain," I describe four typical family situations for TFWs in Canada: living apart from their families, bringing their families with them to Canada, creating new family structures in Canada, and coming to Canada to work for a relative. I use social capital theory to analyze the implications of these different family structures for TFWs in Canada, noting that the most serious personal consequences are for TFWs who work for relatives. I also present a contrasting case: that of a non-TFW who came to Canada under an open work permit and who was thus able to retain and build her social capital, with a positive outcome.

Because there is a global market for labour, it is important to compare the Canadian TFW program with similar programs elsewhere. In chapter 4, "International Comparisons: Canada Is Not the Default Choice," I demonstrate that TFWs make careful comparisons among their opportunities in Canada and a variety of other regions (i.e., the United States, Australia, the European Union, Hong Kong, and the United Arab Emirates). Whereas Canada is generally seen to provide worse remuneration, it is still viewed as an attractive destination because of the working conditions (e.g., less unpaid overtime, safer workplaces, more respect for human rights). Many potential TFWs are also attracted to Canada because of the prospect of obtaining permanent residency, even though not all TFWs are selected to become permanent residents or Canadian citizens when they apply. Moreover, some employers have the mistaken impression that TFWs have few employment options, which may contribute to a belief that it is acceptable to mistreat them.

In chapter 5, "Reluctant or Reckless: Canadian Employers' Use of the TFW Program," I expand on this theme and delve into more detail about employers' experiences with the TFW program. Using a utility analysis framework, I theorize the perceived cost-effectiveness of hiring different types of TFW workers, taking into account both direct costs (e.g., wages), indirect costs (e.g., turnover, absences), and the value added (e.g., employee performance). I also explore employers' perceptions of the Canadian labour market and the TFW program itself. I distinguish between "reluctant" employers – those who prefer to hire Canadians or permanent residents where possible but are resigned to using the TFW program when necessary, and who comply with the TFW guidelines because they see it as a normal cost of doing business – and "reckless" employers – those who use what they perceive as the deficiencies of the TFW program and how it is administered to justify not complying with the TFW regulations.

My research suggests that the TFW program is deeply flawed. Every type of TFW is vulnerable to mistreatment, with some workers especially vulnerable. Third parties, such as agencies or immigration consultants, do not provide adequate support for TFWs or employers, and the one aspect of the Canadian TFW program that is most attractive to applicants – the prospect of permanent residence – is perhaps what makes TFWs the most vulnerable. In the final chapter, "Conclusions: An Enduring Program for Enduring Work?" I suggest that a combination of increased pathways to permanent residency, open work permits, and some administrative changes would offer advantages to TFWs, employers, and Canada.

Interview Methods and Sources

To understand how TFWs experienced their work in Canada, I recruited current and former TFWs as well as employers who hired TFWs who were willing to discuss their experiences. Although these interviews followed a discussion guide, additional questions emerged naturally during the conversation. The interviews were designed to begin with the earliest stages of the employment cycle (e.g., application to the position, possible use of an agency) and included a discussion of daily interactions with managers and co-workers. Because proficiency in English and French was a requirement of the work visa, almost all interviews were conducted in either English or French, with one interview conducted in Spanish.

A total of 103 participants were recruited via advertisements on online community message boards and posts on social media, as well as with snowball sampling. Information about the study was posted or provided, and a discussion ensued with prospective participants to ensure that they were eligible (e.g., held the correct visa, worked in Canada). I sought participants based on purposive sampling to ensure diversity in terms of geography (e.g., different provinces, urban and rural locations); role (e.g., TFWs, managers of TFWs, community organization workers who support TFWs); industry (e.g., food service, agriculture, manufacturing, caregiving); and demographics (e.g., age, career stage, family status, gender). Interviewees were paid CAD$25 to $50 in cash for their participation and were guaranteed confidentiality as well as anonymity if they preferred (e.g., they could use a fictitious name).

Of the fifty-five TFWs, thirty were men and twenty-five were women, with eighteen from the Philippines, eight from Mexico, five from India, three from China, three from South Africa, three from South Korea, two from Morocco, with the remaining thirteen from Bangladesh, Bulgaria, Croatia, France, Guatemala, Ireland, Israel, Jamaica, Japan, New Zealand, and the United States. Fourteen were in-home caregivers, three were SAWP workers, with another agricultural worker in the low-wage stream; thirteen were high-wage workers; and eighteen were low-wage workers. Among the industries represented were professional, scientific, and technical services (five workers); educational services (three workers); finance and insurance (three workers); health care (three workers); manufacturing (three workers); retail trade (three workers); construction (two workers); transportation (two workers); as well as waste management, arts and entertainment, and oil and gas extraction. Twenty TFWs were working in Ontario, thirteen in Alberta, eight in British Columbia, five in Saskatchewan, three in Quebec, three in Newfoundland, and one each in Manitoba, New Brunswick, and Nova Scotia. I also spoke with four workers who held other visas, three spouses of TFWs, and six community support workers (see table 0.2).

Of the thirty-six employers (i.e., managers, and HR representatives) who spoke to me, fourteen were women, and twenty-two were men, and they were part of thirty-three different organizations. Seven owned or managed agricultural enterprises, five worked in companies that provided services, four were families who had hired in-home caregivers, three owned or managed restaurants, two each owned or managed manufacturing companies, educational institutions, silviculture enterprises, slaughterhouses and meatpacking companies, and tourism companies. The remaining companies were retail establishments,

Table 0.2 Description of interview participants (employers and TFWs)

| | TFW streams | | | | | | | | Employers | |
| | Low-wage | | High-wage | | In-home caregiver | | SAWP and other agricultural workers | | | |
Province of arrival	Men	Women	Men	Women	Men	Women	Men	Women	Men	Women
British Columbia	2			2	1	2			8	2
Alberta	8	1	1			2			4	1
Saskatchewan	1			2					1	3
Manitoba			1						1	
Ontario	2	1	1	2	1	7	4		7	6
Quebec			2							
New Brunswick	1					1			1	1
Nova Scotia		1								
Newfoundland	1		2							1
PEI										
Totals	18		13		14		4		36	

publishers, transportation companies, and landscaping companies. Thirteen owners and managers were from Ontario, ten from British Columbia, five from Alberta, four from Saskatchewan, and one each was from Prince Edward Island, New Brunswick, and Quebec.

Interviews with employees were fifty-seven minutes long, on average. Three employee interviews were not recorded. The interviews with the managers, owners, and HR representatives tended to be shorter, and lasted forty-seven minutes on average. We took detailed notes during and after each interview, to supplement the recordings. We conducted most interviews via telephone, with two interviews taking place via Skype and one interview taking place face-to-face. There were approximately 2,150 pages of interview transcripts. Following the interviews, several participants sent me additional documents that related to our conversations. Some TFWs sent me their employment contracts as well as correspondence with their employer, to demonstrate to me clauses in their contracts or the government guidelines their employer had breached. Employers sent me their LMIA forms, to show me how complex the process was. There were about 159 pages of additional materials. These data corroborated the interview data and provided me with more context about participants' experiences.

Subtle Differences in the Types of Mistreatment Endured by Different Groups of TFWs

Academic researchers, community support workers, activists, and business associations readily acknowledge the fact that Canadian temporary foreign workers (TFWs), as a group, are vulnerable to being exploited and mistreated. When I asked managers and business owners about worker mistreatment, they immediately acknowledged that it was a concern – although they usually considered the mistreatment to be anomalous and emphasized that most workers were treated well. When I spoke with TFWs who had had relatively good experiences in Canada, they usually related the story of a friend or relative whose experiences had not been as positive. I spoke with many TFWs for whom this was true as well. The exact proportion of TFWs who are mistreated is difficult to gauge because many TFWs fear repercussions for speaking up; however, it is important to address the scope and seriousness of the mistreatment that *is* reported.

In this chapter, I discuss the mistreatment of workers in all four TFW streams, examining the sometimes minor differences that exist between the experiences of different workers. Because of the overall structure of the TFW program, which only provides closed work permits, all TFWs are vulnerable. However, some individual TFWs have additional risk factors that make them especially vulnerable, and some types of TFWs experience different types of mistreatment because of the nature of their contracts.

Problems with the Seasonal Agricultural Workers Program (SAWP)

As described in the introduction, workers in the Seasonal Agricultural Workers Program comprise the largest group of TFWs in Canada. Several researchers, including Vosko[1] and Binford,[2] explain the tension inherent in this program. On the one hand, the SAWP program is frequently identified as an exemplar because of the benefits that it offers to employers. This program produces a stable workforce with a relatively high proportion of satisfied employers. It also offers many political advantages; having a legal channel for circular migration solves employers' labour supply problems while reducing the likelihood of undocumented workers or politically unpopular increases to immigration levels.

On the other hand, the SAWP program has been heavily criticized for its mistreatment of agricultural workers. The types of mistreatment that these workers face include low pay and wage theft, overwork, tight control over employee movements, lack of access to health care, and substandard housing.[3] Most concerningly, there is considerable evidence that many agricultural workers experience unsafe working conditions. Based on a survey of 100 SAWP workers from Mexico and Jamaica, McLaughlin, Hennebry, and Haines suggest that only a small minority of these workers received training on safe pesticide use (13 per cent) or how to avoid muscle strains and injuries (14 per cent), and any training they received was generally informal and provided by a crew leader or more experienced TFW. They found that although the majority of workers were provided with gloves (75 per cent), very few (less than 5 per cent) were provided with masks or other personal protective equipment.[4]

Several reasons have been proposed to explain why SAWP workers are so vulnerable. All SAWP workers – and indeed all TFWs – are vulnerable because of their "deportability," or the implicit threat of job loss and removal,[5] but some workers have additional risk factors. As several researchers have noted, some SAWP workers have poor English language skills (especially if they are from Mexico), which means that it is more difficult for them to assert their rights when they meet with their supervisor or employer. These workers are unlikely to have social and practical support from family and friends living near the farm where they will be living and working, which means that they may rely heavily on their employer for information about their rights as well as necessities, such as transportation to purchase food and medical supplies. Most significantly, SAWP workers have family members at home who are dependent on their incomes; they are more likely to feel an obligation to maintain positive relationships with their employers – even if they are mistreated – to sustain their employment and to ensure that their incomes are adequate to meet their families' needs.

When I spoke with SAWP workers, they consistently echoed the themes described above. In particular, these workers received little (or no) training, even that relating to occupational health and safety. For example, they were never instructed about their right to know the risks of their job, to refuse unsafe work, or to participate in the health and safety of their workplace. They also rarely received the equipment they needed to do their work safely. They were instead instructed to purchase their own, if they wanted it; using it was never enforced.

I spoke to one SAWP worker from Mexico who worked on a tobacco farm in Ontario. He told me, "The tobacco, the leaves, you know, the branches, it's like having a little dusty, like, like oil, you know, and they coming in your skin. Or the pollen on the floor, you come and you breathe that stuff, and it's coming in your throat. It's like a drug. And then after you start feeling headache, tired, vomit. Sometimes, some people, they falling on the ground because it's strong, you know" (TFW45, male agricultural worker from Mexico, working in Ontario). I asked him if he had had any safety training or if he had been provided with any safety equipment. He replied, "No, they don't care. If you ask them for a mask or something, they say 'You buy your own. When you get paid, you get your own stuff. What you want, you buy.' They say that. But if you don't have it, you have to work like that ... Before when I was working on the tobacco, I got too much sick. Too much sick. I lost maybe twenty-five pounds."

Because of the way the program is structured, all SAWP workers are, by definition, from the Global South. This program draws workers from a limited number of countries (e.g., Mexico, Jamaica). Because of the lack of variation in the demographics of the SAWP workers, it is somewhat challenging to disentangle the extent to which they are vulnerable because of their demographics, and the extent to which they may be especially vulnerable because of other factors. It is therefore instructive to consider the experiences of a non-SAWP agricultural worker from Bulgaria who spoke to me, because he worked alongside SAWP workers and performed similar tasks, although his background was different.

This particular worker experienced significant mistreatment. His employer asked him to pay illegal employment fees, which were characterized as a "union fee," even though, in fact, there was no union. He was also asked to do unsafe tasks such as use chemicals in poorly ventilated enclosed spaces, and his managers isolated him from the other workers when he tried to assert his rights.

This worker's colleagues were also asked to perform dangerous tasks and were not paid overtime. He tried to help them as much as he could. In his words, "I tried to counsel co-workers to not take these deals but when it's the only job that is offered to them, it becomes very exploitative. You say yes because a lot of them aren't in positions of turning it down. A lot of them are there sending money home to their families because they come from a much more destitute part of the world or they don't have stable employment back home or it's a messy situation for some employees" (TFW06, male farm worker from Bulgaria, working in Ontario; NOC 8431, skill level C). He believed that his co-workers were more vulnerable to mistreatment than he was because the consequences of them refusing work were more severe. In particular, he did not have children or other dependents, although he was about the same age as his co-workers. This worker was from Europe and had an undergraduate university degree in computer science, whereas his co-workers were from Mexico and did not have the same level of education. He spoke English confidently, even though it was not his first language, in contrast to his co-workers, who had more difficulty. This worker also had many Canadian social connections, including a sister, friends, and a Canadian girlfriend who lived in a nearby city; his colleagues, in contrast, did not have any local relatives or friends and did not know any Canadians outside their workplace.

In this case, his individual advantages (e.g., education, race, social capital) allowed him to resist the mistreatment that he was faced with. When his employer asked him to perform something that he felt was unsafe or asked him to pay illegal employment fees, he refused. When he was unsure about something that was happening at work, he researched the relevant employment standards or asked his sister or girlfriend for help. He readily acknowledged that his co-workers from Mexico did not have his advantages, which was why he tried to help them.

The experiences of this particular worker suggest that the reasons underlying the mistreatment of SAWP and other TFWs are complex. While any worker technically has the same legal protections, not every worker has the social or human capital to exercise their legal rights, and in some cases the risks inherent in trying to asset their rights are too severe (e.g., termination). Language difficulties, low levels of education, social isolation, and a lack of awareness of employment standards can be considered "risk factors" that make an employee more vulnerable to mistreatment.

Problems with the In-Home
Caregiver Program

The in-home caregiver (formerly the live-in caregiver) program is described in more detail in the introduction. As with the SAWP stream of the TFW program, the in-home caregiver program has received considerable scrutiny from academic researchers and advocacy groups. While the in-home caregiver program is important to the Canadian families who rely on it, there is extensive evidence that in-home caregivers experience significant mistreatment.

One survey, conducted by Oxman-Martinez, Hanley, and Cheung, focused on the experiences of 119 live-in caregivers in Quebec and was supplemented with data from twenty-six focus group participants.[6] Their findings suggested that the vast majority were required to perform tasks that that fell outside the scope of their contracts, including cleaning (88 per cent) and cooking for the family (66 per cent), which may partly explain why about half of their respondents (56 per cent) worked forty-nine hours per week or more. A sizable minority of participants were not paid minimum wage, as required by law (24 per cent), and were not paid appropriately for working on statutory holidays (28 per cent). The fact that the work that these TFWs perform is gendered, in that it is typically completed by women in the domestic sphere, makes this work more invisible and more likely to be undervalued.

The female in-home caregivers who spoke with me identified very similar themes. Almost all caregivers worked more hours than they were paid for, and one was hospitalized for major depression that stemmed from overwork. Likewise, most of the caregivers were asked to perform tasks that were not in their contracts, and that did not directly relate to caring for their clients (e.g., cooking, yardwork, or cleaning). They had little privacy and were usually expected to be on call in case their employers needed them. Moreover, many live-in caregivers were prevented from seeing family or friends, and they found this social isolation to be detrimental to their well-being.

Because of the way in which the in-home caregivers program is structured, these workers are vulnerable in slightly different ways than the SAWP workers. After twenty-four months of employment as an in-home caregiver, these workers are eligible to apply for permanent residence; this right is not afforded to SAWP workers. However, the prospect – but not the affordance – of permanent residency brings with it the same risk factors inherent in "deportability." In-home caregivers are vulnerable because their goal (i.e., permanent residence) is easily dashed by their employers. These workers typically endure the mistreatment to maintain a positive employment relationship.

Moreover, the intimate nature of the work performed by in-home caregivers sets the stage for somewhat more personalized mistreatment, in comparison to what the SAWP workers and other TFWs experience. The psychological abuse many caregivers experienced was very damaging, and it was not expected by less experienced caregivers, who had expected to be treated like a member of the family. For example, I spoke to one in-home caregiver from South Africa who was taken aback by how incurious her employers were about her and how little they cared about her, even though she was looking after their son. Other acts of mistreatment ranged from petty micro-aggressions to violating employment standards; they did not acknowledge her birthday, they called her "a Princess" for asking for a day off, they told her that their son hated her, and they did not pay her promptly or for all the hours she worked (TFW10, female in-home caregiver from South Africa, working in Alberta). In this case, the in-home caregiver was vulnerable because of the inherent power differentials between an employer and an employee with a closed work permit. However, although English was not her first language, she spoke and understood it well, and she was the same race as her employers. Indeed, she was more fortunate than many other in-home caregivers in that she was not supporting any of her extended family; rather, her parents were encouraging her to quit her job and to return home.

An in-home caregiver from the Philippines who spoke to me experienced similar demeaning treatment, but the verbal abuse that she experienced was racialized. Instead of being denigrated as "a Princess" for trying to assert her rights, she was described with a more dehumanizing epithet (i.e., told she looked like a "monkey") and then was forced to cut her hair much shorter in a style she did not like. She was also denied the dignity of being permitted to sleep alone in her own room, as required by the TFW program regulations; the rationale was that she was expected to monitor her elderly employer even while she slept, or instead of sleeping. I asked her how this worked out, and she told me, "She fell from the bed. Though we are sleeping together, I couldn't be awake to catch her. I have to sleep at night. So she fell from the bed, because it was too small and too narrow for her. And then they blamed me" (TFW31, female in-home caregiver from the Philippines, working in Alberta). In this case, the TFW was demeaned and dehumanized, and then fired because she was held to an impossible standard. As with the

SAWP employees, the more risk factors that an employee possesses, the more likely they are to experience more severe mistreatment.

I did speak to two live-in caregivers who had a dramatically different experience. A husband and wife had been hired by a non-profit organization to care for a client with several disabilities. Of all the in-home caregivers who spoke to me, they were the most effusive in expressing their satisfaction with the TFW program.

In this case, the non-profit organization that oversaw their contract arranged for them to be paid above minimum wage, paid for them to receive additional training, ensured that they were paid promptly and in full, and made sure that the workers did not miss breaks or perform tasks that were beyond the scope of their contract. Indeed, they were the only live-in caregivers who did not tell me that they performed unpaid overtime or additional unpaid tasks, and they felt respected as healthcare professionals. It is difficult to infer too much from a single discrepant case, but it is interesting that the most positive in-home caregiver experiences were with a non-profit organization as the employer rather than a family. If this reflects a trend, it suggests that, when predicting mistreatment, the characteristics of the employers bear even more scrutiny than the characteristics of the TFWs. Whereas an individual family that employs a TFW may not have adequate resources (e.g., leadership skills, management training) to manage someone effectively, they may also be biased against workers from the Global South, and they may also be racist or sexist, which may influence how they treat their employees. In contrast, some larger organizations – especially if they have trained personnel who are responsible for managing a workforce – may have some internal checks and balances that can prevent some of the more egregious abuses. The inherent structure of the "home/workplace" where a family employs an individual to work in their home and then determines whether or not they can achieve their goal of citizenship, is inherently uneven; the employer will always have more power than the employee, even if they choose not to exercise it.

Problems with the Low-Wage Program

Unfortunately, the available evidence about the experiences of workers with the low-wage TFW program suggests that these workers are also mistreated. As described in the introduction, these workers work in low-wage and lower-skilled positions, typically in the service sector, such as fast-food restaurants, but also in other industries such as long-term care homes and as security guards. The working conditions in these environments are frequently difficult (i.e., dirty, dangerous, and demeaning) for all employees, and the labour standards in this sector tend not to be widely enforced,[7] but low-wage TFWs face particular concerns. In this sense, low-wage TFWs are, again, "superexploited," to use Valiani's term;[8] they are particularly prone to exploitation because their precarious status is coupled with the lack of value ascribed to the work they perform.

Polanco's qualitative study of Tim Hortons employees[9] is instructive. In her research, she found that low-wage TFWs worked without pay in the (misplaced) hopes that they would be nominated by their employers for the Provincial Nominee Program, and therefore secure permanent residency. Although wage theft is illegal, but not uncommon, among employees in the fast-food restaurant industry, Canadian and permanent resident workers who experience this are able to seek employment elsewhere without completing extensive paperwork and without jeopardizing their citizenship ambitions; they are also more likely to be familiar with their employment rights and where to find alternative employment or resources.

Unlike Canadian low-wage workers, low-wage TFWs have sometimes been required to pay additional fees to their employers.[10] The particular parameters of these illegal fees varied. Sometimes the employer would explicitly require the TFW to pay them a fee to cover the expenses of hiring them instead of a Canadian employee (e.g., the LMIA fee, advertising costs, lawyer fees, and immigration consultant fees). In other cases, TFWs were charged an "administrative fee," an "application fee," or an "ancillary fee." As one community support worker explained to me, "We've had situations where a TFW is employed and the manager comes to them and says you know what we are running out of money, we can't keep you employed for the next two years. And out of desperation the TFW will say I will do anything and, okay, so when I give you your paycheque at the end of two weeks you take it to the bank, you cash it, and you bring back 50 per cent" (SUP01, female community support worker in Alberta). In these instances, the employer is completely violating the terms of the TFW program as well as provincial employment standards, but the low-wage TFW will feel obligated to comply with the request to maintain their employment.

One aspect of the low-wage TFW program that distinguishes it from the high-wage TFW program is the role that employers play in arranging accommodations for their workers. Whereas employers of high-wage TFWs are not at all responsible for providing accommodations, employers of low-wage TFWs must ensure that their workers have access to accommodations where the total rental cost does not exceed 30 per cent of the employee's gross income, and the employer can in fact also become the landlord. These accommodations must meet municipal standards (i.e., comply with municipal building codes), although in practice they may be crowded and unsanitary. Most TFWs told me they preferred to find their own accommodations with roommates of their choice and at a lower cost. Although the provision of affordable housing was perhaps intended to ensure that low-wage TFWs would be paid adequately for the region in which they were working (i.e., to account for the fact that housing in tourism-heavy areas that rely on low-wage TFWs is expensive), many low-wage TFWs found that their living conditions were as exploitative as their working conditions.

Cedillo, Lippel, and Nakache[11] have examined the factors that contribute specifically to the mistreatment of Canadian low-wage TFWs. Their research suggests that the reasons underlying their mistreatment are slightly different from those that affect the SAWP workers and in-home caregivers. As part of a broader study, they interviewed twenty-two current and former skilled and lower-skilled TFWs in the construction, meat processing, hospitality, and fast-food industries. Their analysis suggests that the primary reason why TFWs experience mistreatment (e.g., occupational injuries, employment standards violations such as wage theft) is their dependence on their employers. For several reasons, it was very difficult for them to assert their rights: it was difficult for them to change employers, the TFWs needed their employers' support in the provincial nomination process that would lead to their permanent residency, and they relied on their employers for a place to live. TFWs who were unionized fared a little better, but membership in a union was limited to certain industries.

Interestingly, the distinction between high-wage (higher-skill) and low-wage (lower-skill) TFW streams was sometimes small. The NOC codes are not arbitrary, but there are fine distinctions between some high-wage and low-wage occupations (e.g., baker or chef vs. kitchen helper). Moreover, employers who used the higher-skill TFW program may have equivocated when they listed the relevant NOC codes in their applications, to permit them to hire a higher-skill TFW during periods when access to the lower-skill TFW stream was limited for political reasons (e.g., anti-immigration sentiment or concern about unemployment levels among Canadians). In practice, there was no real guarantee that a worker would be doing what they expected or what was stipulated in their employment contract. The high-wage and low-wage TFW streams may have been introduced to address this issue. However, the distinctions between the new high-wage and low-wage TFW streams may also be small. A worker who is paid $0.01 less than the provincial median will fall under the low-wage TFW program; their counterpart who is paid $0.02 more will fall under the high-wage TFW program and lose some employment benefits and protections (e.g., transportation, housing).

Problems with the High-Wage Program

The academic literature assumes implicitly, and sometimes explicitly, that high-wage or higher-skill TFWs are treated better than low-wage or lower-skill TFWs and TFWs in the in-home caregivers or agricultural programs. For example, Fudge and Tham suggest that the temporary nature of a wealthy or skilled migrant worker's visa is not sufficient to make them vulnerable to labour exploitation. They note specifically that "nurses in Australia on a skilled workers visa are unlikely to be vulnerable to exploitation by their employers even though their residence in the host country is temporary."[12] Likewise, Strauss and McGrath state that "highly skilled workers and entrepreneurs may well experience significant advantages in the labour markets of host countries. Many national immigration regimes, including Canada's ... are increasingly oriented towards attracting these migrants, in some cases offering preferential access to citizenship to mobile elites who are seen as the human equivalent of footloose capital."[13] Strauss and McGrath also note that "creative and high-tech workers on flexible contracts ... may have relatively little in common with the migrant workers who labour in poorly paid jobs to feed, clean, and care for the children of more highly-paid workers."[14] Indeed, the TFWs in the in-home caregiver[15] and agricultural programs are sometimes described as "second-class" workers,[16] which implies that the high-wage[17] TFWs must therefore be "first-class" and receive commensurably better treatment.

The general assumption among academic researchers appears to be that high-wage TFWs are admitted to Canada as part of a targeted immigration strategy that is designed to attract new citizens, while the other types of TFWs are tolerated temporarily as non-citizens.[18] The high-wage TFWs are said to be considered "proto-Canadians" and are thus assumed to be treated well, while the other types of TFWs are considered "non-Canadians" and are therefore vulnerable.[19] Indeed, among the TFWs that I spoke with, there was also a general tendency to believe that high-wage workers faced few risks in Canada and would not be mistreated. For example, one high-wage TFW, a communications director from Ireland working in Quebec,[20] found that he was treated very well and ascribed this to his status as a high-wage TFW from Europe rather than from the Global South. As he explained it: "There seems to be a steady stream of stories coming out of that region where foreign workers under this program, particularly low-wage foreign workers, are asked to do things by their employer that they aren't contracted to do. And they face either implicit or explicit threats that if they don't do this, then they'll face hardship. Either them or their family will face hardship" (TFW42, male communications director from Ireland working in Quebec; NOC 5121, skill level A). He believed that the high-wage TFW program, unlike the other streams, was a safe and desirable option for skilled workers who were interested in moving to Canada. As with the agricultural worker from Bulgaria, he felt that others were far more vulnerable than he was.

The Canadian high-wage TFW program has not been studied as extensively as the other programs have, but evidence from the Australian Temporary Work (Skilled) visa (subclass 457)[21] is instructive. As with the Canadian high-wage TFWs, these workers' wages had to meet a set threshold, and their employer had to demonstrate that the position could not be filled locally. Unfortunately, in her analysis of legal decisions related to skilled temporary workers between 1996 and 2017, Boucher notes that there was conclusive evidence that some of these workers were mistreated. She catalogued the types of mistreatment that these workers experienced, and found that the most common form of mistreatment was underpayment (37 per cent of cases), followed by unfair dismissal (15 per cent). However, there were also instances of workplace injury and workplace safety violations.[22] These findings are similar to those reported by Cedillo and her colleagues, who investigated the experiences of both skilled and low-skilled TFWs in Canada.[23]

In my research, I interviewed twelve high-wage TFWs, and many of them reported mistreatment. I report these findings in more detail because this topic has thus far received little attention. Much of the high-wage TFWs' mistreatment is remarkably similar to what TFWs in the other programs have experienced. However, there are also some subtle differences.

Required to Perform Additional Tasks Not Specified in the Contract

According to the TFW program's guidelines, high-wage TFWs must be recruited to perform a specific job with clearly defined duties and responsibilities. The rationale is that an employer cannot advertise for one type of employee and then ask the person hired to perform a different set of tasks. The TFWs need to know what they are agreeing to when they agree to come to Canada to work and the employer should avoid a situation where Canadians would have applied for the position if they had known what the actual duties were.

The employer therefore loses some flexibility by hiring a TFW instead of a Canadian, but presumably accepts this as one of the trade-offs in pursuing this type of staffing. Of the employers who spoke with me about their experiences with the higher-skill TFW stream, several noted that the available NOC codes did not accurately represent the types of tasks that they needed to hire someone for. In some cases, the available NOC codes were too general and could not capture the complexity of the job. For example, no NOC code is available for "master cheesemaker"; the closest might be for "process control and machine operators, food and beverage processing (NOC C)," but that code does not accurately reflect the education and training needed for small-batch cheesemaking, and would not enable a high-wage TFW to be hired. In this case, the cheesemaker would need to choose an alternative code (e.g., farm supervisors and specialized livestock workers; NOC B). That code still does not closely reflect these work-ers' duties because they would not normally work with livestock or supervise other employees, but it would have permitted a high-wage TFW to be hired.

The lack of nuance in the NOC categories was a double-edged sword. On the one hand, several employers seemed to purposely misclassify a TFW as a manager to meet the federal TFW program's guidelines for hiring a higher-skill TFW. The TFWs who were hired under these circum-stances were disappointed with the scope of the duties that they were actually permitted to do, especially because many had extensive quali-fications and credentials that they felt were being underused. On the other hand, several TFWs reported to me that, in fact, they were taking on the duties of a manager but they were not being paid accordingly because their NOC code could not accommodate this. TFWs were also frustrated when they believed they were prohibited from applying for internal promotions to managerial positions because corporate policies prevented them from doing so (i.e., only Canadian citizens could be managers). However, in these instances the corporate policy was likely aligned with the federal guidelines that required the TFWs to remain in the precise job for which they had been hired.

A frequent theme among the high-wage TFWs was that that they were initially hired to perform one job, but then were actually expected to do something else as part of their duties. Sometimes they were asked to perform several different jobs concurrently or work at several different locations, in violation of their contract. This is again against the federal TFW guidelines because it mischaracterizes the work available, which may prevent a Canadian from applying for that job, and it gives TFW applicants a biased impression of what the job will entail. For example, a highly skilled baker in Alberta I spoke with explained to me that he was working at three different locations of the same chain restaurant, in violation of his contract and the TFW program's guidelines. As he explained, "the owner told him look I have a good slave, his name is [TFW's name]. I bring him from Morocco, just give him all the product for three stores, he will do it. He will not speak up. And this is what happened I did it for four or five months when I go with them. Or more than that because they take me from [restaurant name] to [location] in January, so that's more than eight months" (TFW11, male from Morocco, working in Alberta as a baker; NOC Code B).

In this regard, the experiences of this worker were not dissimilar to those of the TFWs I spoke with who were working in the other streams. The TFWs were expected to adapt to the needs of their employers, whether or not the new duties reflected those stipulated in their contracts.

The qualifications or credentials of the high-wage TFWs did not insulate them from mistreatment. Indeed, their more advanced skills may have made them more susceptible to being pressured to perform additional tasks or duties because they were so experienced and competent. For example, one post-doctoral fellow from Algeria who spoke to me was asked to take on the duties of a lab technician – in addition to his own research duties – because the lab technician and some other employees had quit. The post-doctoral fellow was able to do these tasks because of his prior laboratory experience while working in France and Poland, but they conflicted with his primary duties: generating ideas for new research projects and writing research papers.

Oddly, this worker met with his supervisor only three or four times during his eight-month contract; much of their communication was via emails sent through his supervisor's secretary. He found that he was significantly hindered by his supervisor's hands-off management style; his co-workers refused to teach him how to use some of the specialized laboratory equipment, and his boss did not require them to do so. He also felt that the other workers received more interesting and developmental work assignments. This behaviour is different from what workers in the SAWP, in-home caregiver, and low-wage programs reported, but it was significantly damaging to his career prospects. To secure future contracts or permanent employment, he needed to publish academic research papers and learn new analytic methods, but he was denied this opportunity. Although he had come to Canada to further his career, his job as a TFW ended up being detrimental to his future prospects.

Underpaid Relative to What Was Promised in the Contract

The TFW program's guidelines stipulate that all TFWs must be paid the local median wage for the region and occupation (as determined by the appropriate NOC code) and that managers must comply with other provincial and federal wage guidelines.[24] The goal is to ensure that employers hire TFWs only when qualified Canadians cannot be found to do this work at a fair wage – and not that Canadians cannot be found to do this work at an artificially low wage – and to avoid depressing Canadian workers' wages because of an influx of foreign labour. These guidelines are clearly stated in the application process, and several employers I spoke with explained that a failure to comply would lead to an application being denied.

Unfortunately, workers in the high-wage TFW program are also vulnerable to unilateral (and illegal) changes to their wages and contracts. Contracts could be renewed after they expired, but any new contracts were subject to the same strict government rules and regulations as the original contracts (e.g., the employer needed to obtain a new LMIA and the employee still needed to be paid at or above the local median wage for that occupation). I had several conversations with workers who had to decide how they would react to a "bait and switch" contract breach, where they came to work for a particular employer because of the provisions offered in their employment contract only to have the contract changed after they started working. Because they wanted to maintain their employment with that particular employer, they felt that they could not quit or complain about this mistreatment.

For example, I spoke with a medical sonographer from China. She had been working as a physician in China, and her qualifications made her eligible for a job as a medical sonographer that the employer was staffing through the higher-skill TFW stream.[25] She chose to work in Saskatchewan because of the opportunity to potentially become a permanent resident through the provincial nominee program. When she first arrived, everything seemed fine. However, over time she found that her hours were being cut back; some days she would be sent home early without pay because patients had cancelled and there was little for her to do. The changes to her work hours were in violation of her contract, which guaranteed her a minimum number of hours of work per week; she was willing to endure this because her hourly rate was maintained as promised. However, she then told me that her boss wanted to renew her contract at a lower rate of pay. This new contract would violate the TFW program's guidelines because her wages would be below the local median for her occupation.

> I came here with one-year work permit. After I work for six months, I started to ask him if he would like to keep me for more years ... He told he wants to reduce 30 per cent of my payment to continue my work contract ... Like he said, if I want to work for him longer, more than one year, and if he wants to he doesn't want to pay me as much as the first year. He reduces 30 per cent of my income. The first year he keep all the rules from the contract. Because I'm a foreigner, so he ask me to work for him, I got a Labour Market Assessment something. Do you know what I'm talking? I ask him if he would like to keep me longer. He said that my contract was one year. If I want to work for him for the other year or the other two, three years, he doesn't want to pay me as much as right now, as much as before. He reduce 30 per cent of my payment ... if I want to immigrate I have to agree. (TFW56, female sonographer from China, working in Saskatchewan; NOC 3216, skill level B)

In this example, the worker was vulnerable because her employer knew that she wanted to immigrate to Canada and become a permanent resident. To do this through the Saskatchewan provincial nominee program, she needed to demonstrate consistent employment in an in-demand occupation. The federal regulations stipulate that the employer must keep the working conditions (i.e., wages, hours of work, duties) the same throughout the contract, and they must match what was originally granted during the course of the Labour Market Impact Assessment (LMIA), as approved by the government. Employers cannot change the contract, partly because the employee is also beholden to it.

Overall, the high-wage TFWs may be more likely to face unilateral wage reductions than the other types of TFWs because their wages are higher than the minimum wage. For example, the sonographer's wages were initially high enough that the employer could lower her wages considerably (in this case 30 per cent) without falling below the minimum wage for Saskatchewan.[26] Presumably, the employer

perceived that paying a worker below minimum wage would be egregious enough to trigger a complaint to the government that could lead
to significant fines or an ineligibility to use the TFW program in the
future, whereas they perceived that simply breaching the contract and
paying the worker less than the contract stipulated was tacitly permitted. In contrast, TFWs who only make minimum wage (e.g., in-home
caregivers, kitchen helpers, or counter attendants) would not face
this specific type of mistreatment, although these workers frequently
find that they are expected to work longer hours either unpaid or at
rates that do not take overtime into account.

Assuming this sonographer was working full-time and paid the
median sonographer wage in Saskatchewan of \$36.00/hour, reducing
her wages by 30 per cent, or by \$10.80/hour, would garner her employer
a savings of approximately \$22,464/year. In this regard, the high-wage
TFW was an attractive target, because of her high wages.

Health and Safety Violations

All employees in Canada, including TFWs, have the right to know about
the safety hazards in their workplaces, the right to participate in decisions about the safety of their workplaces, and the right to refuse unsafe
work.[27] Some of the high-wage TFWs who spoke with me worked in
environments with minimal hazards, for example, white-collar jobs, as
accountants or computer programmers. They did not receive specific
safety training, but they did not perceive there to be any particular
hazards in their workplaces, and they did not report being injured or
ill as a result of their work.

However, some high-wage TFWs told me their work environments
were unsafe. These TFWs were often employed in restaurants or industrial settings (i.e., not in white-collar jobs) and faced a wide variety of
hazards. It is important to note that workplaces that had cut corners or
had mistreated workers in one regard (e.g., did not provide breaks as
stipulated in a contract) were also frequently delinquent in protecting
their workers. I asked a baker from Jamaica whether he had received
any training. He told me, "I got safety training like three or four months
before my contract was up. That's how I got my safety training. That was
a little bit late ... Yeah so that thing is mandatory. There's a lot of stuff
that I just got a walk through, I don't know about the first set of foreign
workers that were there before me because there was some Jamaican
also there that they started working a couple months before me. And
it was a different manager at that time. But when I start working, I

just got a walk through" (TFW13, male baker from Jamaica, working in Alberta; NOC 6332, skill level B).

Although the baker was experienced and had a strong understanding of safe work practices, he should still have received safety training when he began work instead of several months afterwards. The equipment and processes would have been different at his new bakery, and it would have been important to show him how to report injuries and receive first aid. By providing this baker with safety training several months after he began work, the employer failed to provide a safe work environment. This particular worker found that the employer engaged in a general pattern of negligence: he did not provide the safety training, he did not provide legally mandated work breaks, and he did not provide the work uniform the worker had been promised as part of his contract. When he became a permanent resident, he quit working for this employer even though he did not have another job lined up.

Some high-wage TFWs said they were discouraged from reporting injuries or illnesses that were interfering with their work. One of these workers was a foreman for an oil and gas company in Alberta.[28] An older man, originally from Boston, he was working as a TFW to pay off some household debts so that he and his wife could retire. He had considerable experience as an ironworker, and generally found the work site to be safe, in terms of the equipment that was provided and the processes that were followed. However, he faced considerable pressure to continue working even when he was sick, even though being sick would make it more difficult for him to safely execute his duties, and even though his illness was contagious. He likely contracted his illness because of the close living conditions in the "camps" or accommodations provided to workers by the company, and it was likely exacerbated by the physically demanding work and work schedule (i.e., twelve hours a day for ten days, followed by ten days of rest). As he explains:

> I got sick a few times. Oh at [location] I got sick like you read about. There was some nasty bug going around camp and I was sick for probably a week ... I told my boss. See I was a foreman at the time, I told my boss and I told him I wanted to go to the doctor. He said look [name] if you go to the doctor they're just going to send you back to camp and you're not going to make any money. He kind of discouraged me from even reporting it. I was a little bit disappointed in that. That was the time I had pneumonia. (TFW14, male ironworker foreman from USA, working in Alberta; NOC Code B)

Alberta's provincial employment standards at the time entitled all workers to at least five unpaid sick days without jeopardizing their employment. The fact that this worker was highly skilled, very experienced, and well paid did not protect him from pressure to continue working and to avoid reporting his illness. Indeed, because of the intense production schedule and his position of responsibility, he may have faced additional pressure to work. This particular episode was quite damaging to his health, and he stopped working shortly thereafter. This mistreatment was similar to that reported by the agricultural workers I spoke with; they also felt that they needed to continue working even if they were sick or injured. This perception is well documented in the research literature.[29] Indeed, several managers reiterated the importance of employees who were "reliable," "had a good attitude," and were "willing to work." While in some instances these statements applied to a willingness to undertake normal (if undesirable) job duties, in other instances they applied to workers who had sustained an injury that the manager considered too minor to interfere with the production schedule. These managers also expressed skepticism about the abilities of doctors to accurately gauge if a worker was ready to return to normal work duties. They believed that it was appropriate to repeatedly ask the worker if they were able to do various and incrementally more difficult tasks once they returned to work.

The high-wage TFWs did not appear to be targeted for unsafe work practices, relative to the Canadian workers. However, the high-wage TFWs were somewhat more vulnerable than Canadian employees because their past experiences may not have prepared them for the specific hazards of a new workplace; despite their experience and high skill level, they may have had to operate new equipment and learn new processes.[30] Like the TFWs in the other streams, the high-wage TFWs were also vulnerable; because they had closed work permits, they could not easily quit and go to work for a safer competitor.

Paying Additional Fees

Like the low-wage TFWs, the high-wage TFWs reported being required to pay kickbacks or additional fees to their employers, in clear violation of the terms of the TFW program as well as provincial labour standards. Unfortunately, this phenomenon was fairly widespread among both high-wage and low-wage TFWs. I spoke with one higher-skill TFW, a cook from Japan,[31] who nervously told me that he had had to reimburse his employer the fees that the employer had paid to the government. As he explains:

I don't know how much I can talk to you about how I got the closed work permit. But like my employer had to pay a certain amount of fee to the government. And then I also had to pay for the application fees to the government. So like both parties had to pay. And then my company paid for the government too for my applications.

[Yes? And then did they want you to pay them back?]

Yeah. I paid them back too.

[So you paid the company too? So you paid the government and the company for the application?]

Yeah, but it's kind of like a secret thing, so I don't want to say it to anybody. (TFW55, male cook from Japan, working in Manitoba; NOC 6322, skill level B)

In this case, the fees would be for the Labour Market Impact Assessment (LMIA), which would amount to $1,000. It is illegal for employers to pass these costs directly onto their employees, but the practice is not uncommon. Typically, an arrangement is made before the company makes the LMIA application. The TFW, who may already be in Canada, then cashes their paycheque and remits a cash fee to the manager. The amount of the fee varies, but it is usually over $1,000. This payment to the employer would be in addition to any expenses that the TFW incurred in finding the job (e.g., airfare if it is not included in the contract, fees paid to recruitment agencies).

In other instances, the TFWs were charged several "fees." For example, I spoke with a videographer[32] from Croatia who was hired to work for a skydiving company. She was charged for her training (in violation of labour standards), which caused her significant financial hardship. To earn enough money to cover her monthly expenses she agreed to do additional work cleaning the airplanes and working as a seamstress. This extra work was unrelated to the original job that she had been hired to do (in violation of the federal TFW program's guidelines). To work as a seamstress, she had to pay her employer rent for a sewing room (in violation of the guidelines). Eventually, she quit this employer and found a new job, where she was asked to pay her new employer $4,000 in fees (in violation of the guidelines and well in excess of the $1,000 cost of the LMIA). After her new job began, her wages were lowered (in violation of the guidelines). She explains:

I agreed to do some work on the side, to make money for my training, and I did cleaning job. But he later on asked me to clean the airplanes. I had to come to work for lower money. I had to rent sewing room. I had to pay $300 monthly plus taxes to rent the room where I would actually sew, even though I was employee. So for a year and a half, he was charging me for $300 per month to rent the room at his premises to do my sewing work. You can't ... I was employee, right? With needing work as well, I found another employer who knew exactly that they are my last chance to regulate my status. And I pay representatives and all expenses related to LMIA, which was $4,000. When I obtained work permit, they lowered my wages. (TFW30, female videographer from Croatia, working in Ontario; NOC 5222, skill level B)

Although many TFWs in different streams were extorted in similar ways, workers in the high-wage TFW program may make somewhat more attractive targets because they are perceived to have the resources to provide the requested payments. As with the other TFW workers, however, they have difficulty exercising their rights. Because they have closed work permits, it is difficult for high-wage TFWs to change employers, and they need to maintain continuous employment in an in-demand occupation to be eligible for the provincial nominee programs, which they typically need to pursue if they are to achieve their goals of becoming permanent residents.

Why Are Skilled or High-Wage TFWs Mistreated?

In Boucher's analysis of Australian skilled temporary workers, she examines which worker characteristics were associated with mistreatment. She finds that gender was not a significant predictor of worker mistreatment, although she acknowledges that female temporary workers may be less likely than their male counterparts to report incidents of sexual harassment, because of the stigma of these events. Rather, Boucher's results suggest that individuals from China and the Philippines, representing 26 per cent and 14 per cent of all cases, were more likely than other workers to be mistreated despite comprising only 6.5 per cent and 7.9 per cent of the skilled temporary workers in Australia, respectively. She concludes that "employment violations for individuals from these countries are based at least in part upon an individual's ethnic background."[33] These findings are echoed in the experiences of the agricultural worker from Bulgaria described above; he found that his racialized co-workers experienced worse mistreatment than he did, and also that they were less able to defend themselves against the actions of their employer. His racialized coworkers also had language barriers that prevented them from fully understanding and exercising their rights.

The racialized high-wage TFWs who spoke to me did seem to receive worse treatment than those who were not racialized. Some cases echoed the ways in which TFWs in the SAWP stream were treated. For example, the laboratory researcher whose experiences I describe above was Black, unlike his co-workers. He was told to work longer hours without pay, or else his employment would be terminated. He said, "The boss came to me and said look if you don't accelerate your job I will fire you. And he said okay I have Chinese students – I never saw these Chinese students actually – who work until 8 p.m. and they work during weekends. I said what? This guy wants me during weekends. Pay me extra hours and I will work for you for this period" (TFW20, male post-doctoral fellow from France/Algeria, working in Quebec; NOC 4011, skill level A). Even though he was a high-wage TFW, the fact that this researcher's supervisor threatened to replace him specifically with workers of another ethnicity echoes the management style of some farmers, as described by Binford and Preibisch, who pit Mexican and Jamaican SAWP workers against each other.[34] As with many SAWP workers, this high-wage TFW was held to an unreasonable standard of productivity, with a threat that he would be replaced if he could not meet this standard. His manager seemed to be stereotyping the abilities and motivations of different racialized groups, and this high-wage TFW had to cope with the manifestations of these biases.

As with the low-wage TFWs, the high-wage TFWs were motivated to endure mistreatment to please their employers, because they feared that they would be fired. Because they held closed work permits, they did not have the option of leaving a bad employment situation to work for a Canadian competitor. They were very aware of the ways in which their mistreatment violated the terms of their contracts and the TFW program regulations, but they felt unable to resist or report their employers' behaviours.

Conclusion

All TFWs in Canada – including those in the high-wage program – have closed work permits; they cannot easily change employers. Employers know this, so the workers are vulnerable. As Skrivankova noted in her work on the continuum of exploitation, "visas being tied to a particular employer creates a dissonance of power and seriously limits the negotiating power of a worker."[35] Above and beyond a base level of vulnerability, some workers have additional risk factors because of their individual differences (e.g., language skills, education, credentials, race, citizenship in the Global South).

Another, more mundane, contributing factor that has been over-looked is the poor leadership skills of some of the TFW managers. The practice of abusive or destructive leadership has been widely studied in organizational behaviour and human resources management literatures. Although some research has focused on what makes some employees more vulnerable (e.g., gender, personality, performance),[36] a growing literature is considering the attributes of the leaders themselves. The research thus far suggests that a variety of factors predict whether a leader will be abusive, including narcissism and lack of political skills,[37] low emotional intelligence,[38] and sleep deprivation,[39] as well as high levels of depressive symptoms, anxiety, and workplace alcohol consumption.[40]

A picture, therefore, emerges of an anxious manager who is unskilled at leading (but likely to be proficient in producing the service or product that his company offers) and who faces significant pressure to maintain or increase the profitability of the company. Because of a lack of leadership training and skills, this manager will have difficulty recruiting and retaining Canadian employees – especially if the company is unwilling or unable to pay above-market wages. If the company then turns to the TFW program to meet their employment needs, the underlying issue of poor leadership skills will remain unaddressed.

It is important to acknowledge that many of the managers I spoke with only used the TFW program reluctantly and sincerely felt they needed it to find suitable workers. These managers were very willing to hire Canadians and treated all their workers at least reasonably well. However, a pattern also emerged of some managers exhibiting consistently poor leadership skills. They did not plan ways of meeting their staffing requirements well in advance, they did not treat their workers respectfully, and they seemed to prefer that their employees be dependent on them to ensure that they would remain "loyal" (i.e., not quit when they were mistreated) and maintain a "good attitude" (i.e., not complain about any mistreatment). These managers were not focused on creating a mutually beneficial relationship with their employees, and they were generally dissatisfied with the available Canadian workforce. It was not surprising to me that these managers had difficulty recruiting qualified Canadians to work for them, given their leadership style and their lack of planning. I provide more information about what I term reluctant and reckless users of the TFW program in chapter 5.

This pattern is perhaps emblematic of a broader trend in the quality of employment in Canada. As Fudge and Tham explain, the quality and conditions of work have generally diminished in certain sectors (e.g., food services), enforced by minimum wage rates and provincial labour standards.[41] These conditions make it more difficult for employers to recruit Canadian employees, so they demand more TFWs. The continued existence of TFWs, then, acts as a buffer against market pressures to increase wages or improve working conditions. Although this phenomenon has been documented in the low-wage sectors, it may also exist in other occupations. Employers have few incentives to raise wages and invest in equipment or processes that improve the quality of the work environment when there is a ready supply of less expensive foreign labour.

2

Enduring Problems with Agents

One might think that agencies and immigration consultants could solve some of the problems identified in the previous chapter. For example, an independent broker could conceivably help temporary foreign workers (TFWs) to navigate a complex bureaucracy and help them to counterbalance the bargaining power of employers. However, my research suggests that agents themselves are a source of mistreatment. Agents, such as employment agencies and immigration consultants, act in their own interests, which are typically at odds with the interests of the parties (i.e., principals) who hire them. There is a paradox here. TFWs and employers hire agents because they lack the expertise to navigate Canadian bureaucracy. Their lack of expertise means that they are equally unable to assess and monitor the actions of the agents that they hire.

In this chapter, I discuss the problems faced by both TFWs and employers who contract the services of employment agencies and immigration consultants. I draw on agency theory to examine the difficulties inherent in the use of an agent, in terms of goal incongruence, information asymmetries, and differing attitudes toward risk. I also consider the role of external regulation, and how this affects agents' behaviour. The short-term nature of the contracts exacerbates the problems posed by information asymmetries and competing interests; by the time a TFW or employer realizes that a particular agent is mistreating them, the fees have been paid and the contract has ended.

What do Agencies and Immigration Consultants do?

Employment agencies or recruiters match TFWs to available jobs, while immigration consultants help employers and TFWs with paperwork.[1] Canadian employment agencies are not allowed to charge individuals any fees in exchange for finding them a job; all costs are borne by the employer.[2] These recruitment costs are in addition to the legitimate expenses that the employer must bear as part of the process to apply to and use the TFW program. They include the standard fee to apply for a Labour Market Impact Assessment (LMIA) from the federal government;[3] any costs associated with advertising the open position nationally (i.e., to show that a qualified Canadian is not available); housing (for agricultural workers hired under the Seasonal Agricultural Worker Program (SAWP) and most in-home caregivers); and the worker's airfare (in the case of the in-home caregiver program).[4] Recruitment and selection also include several additional costs; employers that outsource this HR function are paying to reduce the time that they need to spend reviewing applications and interviewing candidates. However, even when employers work with an international employment agency, they are still likely to need to interview finalists either in person or via videoconferencing.

What Do Agencies and Immigration Consultants Promise?

The use of Canadian employment agencies and immigration consultants should ideally make recruiting, selecting, and settling TFWs more efficient and effective for both workers and employers. The government protocols are complicated and ever-changing but must be strictly adhered to, and first-time users may find them confusing, especially if they lack legal training or have difficulty understanding English or French. Because agencies and immigration consultants specialize in the legal parameters of the Canadian TFW program, it is possible for them to provide relevant information and services efficiently. However, this specialized knowledge can lead to information asymmetries whereby the agency or immigration consultant bears little risk for any mistakes that they make, and the clients have little warning or recourse.

Agency Theory

Agency theory is a useful lens through which to examine the inherent and inevitable problems in the use of agents, such as employment agencies and immigration consultants. This theory is widely used in economics and organizational behaviour to understand agency relationships, those that exist between the party (i.e., the principal) who delegates the work (i.e., the agent) and the party who performs that work.[5] In the context of the Canadian TFW program, agency theory can be used to understand two relationships: first, the relationship between employment agencies or immigration consultants and the TFWs who seek their services, and second, the relationship between the employment agencies or immigration consultants and the employers who pay for their services.

Agency theory identifies two problems that are inherent in any agency relationship.[6] The first problem, known as the agency problem, arises because the desires or goals of the principal and agent are in conflict, and it is difficult or expensive for the principal to verify what the agent is actually doing. The second problem is that of risk sharing. This arises when the principal and the agent have different attitudes toward risk, and thus prefer different actions.

Problems with Agencies and Immigration Consultants, from TFWs' Point of View

The problems faced by TFWs who use employment agencies or immigration consultants have been described in detail by Villegas in her account of illegalized Mexican labourers who travelled to Canada in search of work. She explains that although the dominant image of immigration facilitators is of smugglers assisting those who seek to work without a visa or work permit, the scope of these agents is broader and includes providing a range of assistance to workers entering Canada. Villegas explains that migrant workers seek assistance because of the uncertainty inherent in navigating a complex process, but then face problems of confiscated travel documents, extortion, and threats of deportation.[7] Extending these findings, I consider the structural problems inherent in principal-agent relationships and how they affect TFWs' experiences.

Agents and TFWs Have Different Goals

The goals of employment agencies and immigration consultants are markedly different than those of community support organizations, despite some superficial similarities. Although each of these groups may provide legal, settlement, and practical assistance to TFWs, employment agencies and immigration consultants – like all businesses – exist to generate profits for their owners or investors. Their goals are thus also at odds with the goals of TFWs, who are seeking employment in Canada and who often have a secondary goal of becoming permanent residents.

It therefore behooves employment agencies and immigration consultants to promise as much as possible, as a way to attract more potential TFWs and to distinguish themselves from their competitors. In addition to securing employment for TFWs, some agencies advertise that they monitor or enforce the employment contract and provide other resources to help with the transition to working in Canada, including picking up the TFW at the airport and helping them to apply for a social insurance number (SIN), bank account, health card, or driver's licence. Some agencies actually do provide these services, but many fail to deliver on their promises.

Because their goal is to maximize profits, employment agencies and immigration consultants are motivated to charge TFWs for their services, even though this is not permitted. Indeed, there are ongoing reports that many TFWs are charged exorbitant fees[8] to come to Canada to work as retail workers,[9] restaurant staff,[10] in-home caregivers,[11] farm labourers,[12] or truck drivers.[13] The fees that some TFWs are illegally required to pay to their employment agencies are in addition to any illegal fees charged by their employers[14] (as discussed in chapter 1). In some cases, the services provided by the agencies were more akin to human smuggling or trafficking than assisting with employment searching or paperwork.[15] As a community support worker in Alberta explained to me:

> We had one case where there was a man from Sri Lanka that had been treated badly – $36,000 actually, was his story … But he had paid $18,000 to come here himself and the agent took the deed to his land and his wife and daughter's passports until he paid the additional $18,000 to bring them. He got a deal, don't you know, two for the price of one. Yeah! Isn't that great? He actually, physically, had to drive to Edmonton to take possession of them … after he handed over the rest of the money, then his wife and daughter were released to him. (SUP01, female community support worker in Alberta)

Given the steep price extracted from the TFWs, one might assume that the agency or immigration consultant would then provide excellent service as a way of fulfilling the contract. Unfortunately, this isn't always the case. Despite having the authority to act on behalf of a TFW, an agency can undermine the best interests of the worker. For example, one nanny explained to me that she needed to find a new employer quickly because of an abusive situation. She decided to sign up with an agency that her friend had recommended. However, the agency pressured her into signing a contract with a new employer that required her to pay for her own food and lodging (against federal guidelines) and to work twelve-hour days (also against federal guidelines). As the nanny explained:

> So since I have no choice at that time, because I really wanted to quit my job with my first employer, so I don't have any choice but to accept their conditions that I need to pay for the board and lodging. And then, what else? It should be only eight hours, but then again they want me to work twelve hours a day. They included it on the contract, but with the LMIA program, board and lodging should not be included there. But then again, they said that their food is not cheap, they're buying organic stuff, so oh, okay, so I don't have choice at that time but to pay. So they asked me to pay for the board and lodging.
>
> So, yeah, I told the agency at that time that I will not accept the job, but they said, the employer is waiting for you to come, and then they're very happy, like that, like that, and everything, okay. So I said yes. [But then] I talked to my agent and asked her why is this? Why are they not paying me my overtime? And she said there's nothing you [can do], it's like you can't do anything about it because you already signed a contract. It's like that. It's a kind of verbal agreement, like that, since you agreed to work in their household. (TFW33, female in-home caregiver from the Philippines, working in Alberta and Ontario; NOC 4411, skill level C)

In this instance, the TFW switched from one bad employer to another. The agency pressured the TFW to accept poor working conditions, and it did not explain the TFW's rights, mediate the dispute with the employer (e.g., to receive additional pay for the extra hours that were worked), find the TFW a new employer, or explain to her how she might report the employer to the federal government.

According to agency theory, this treatment is unsurprising. The employment agency's goal was to place the TFW with an employer so it could collect its fee. Having done so, it would be unlikely for them to expend any more resources in providing additional services to the TFW. Moreover, they would not wish to risk alienating the employer, partly because they had paid their fee and also because there are far more available TFWs than there are employers. An alienated employer is far more difficult to replace. Furthermore, the employer is more likely to be a repeat client; once the TFW has applied for and received permanent residence status – or quit and sought another position elsewhere – there is a possibility that the client will return to the agency and request a new contract. In any dispute between a TFW and an employer, the agent is incentivized to side with the employer.

TFWs Cannot Verify What Agents Are Doing

One of the central problems in the principal-agent working relationship is that the principal has incomplete information about what the agent is actually doing. The agent is hired because of their specialized knowledge or expertise, and thus the principal cannot easily verify the appropriateness of their actions. Because of the significant information asymmetry between TFWs and employment agencies and immigration consultants, I observed many instances of TFWs' interests being undermined by the agents they had hired.

Several TFWs paid fees to employment agencies or immigration consultants but then discovered that their agencies had made significant errors in the paperwork, preventing them from being hired by a company that wanted to employ them. One graphic designer in Ontario[16] explained that she had found an immigration consultant through her employment agency. She trusted the consultant because of a shared language and culture, but this trust was misplaced. As she explained: "I decided to go with her because she's Latin, so she speaks Spanish, and that kind of influenced me a little bit in my decision. And I decided to trust in her, and she did make a few mistakes while applying. So the mistakes were weird because they were where she posted the job as. They have always worked for her, or apparently they have always worked for her, but they didn't work in my case. They didn't work in my advantage" (TFW43, female graphic designer from El Salvador, working in Ontario; NOC 5241, skill level B).

In this case, the TFW was relying on her immigration consultant to work with her employer to document that her occupation (web designer) was undersupplied in the employer's region. This information was necessary because to qualify for the LMIA, the employer's company needed to demonstrate that the TFW was filling a job vacancy for which there were no qualified Canadians. However, the errors made by the immigration consultant led to the LMIA being rejected. This phenomenon is also described by Villegas, who further notes that the agents expend little effort in advocating for their clients because they may then

charge additional fees if an appeal is needed.[17] Agents are motivated to
extend the legal proceedings as much as possible, because it is profitable
for them; they do not need to worry about building a professional
reputation because there is an ample supply of potential TFWs who
will seek to hire them because they share a language and an ethnicity.

Often, TFWs use an agency or immigration consultant because
they do not believe that they can navigate the bureaucracy on their
own. For example, one convenience store cashier had worked with an
agency that had been investigated by the RCMP for stealing personal
information from Canadians and then using that information to create
fake employment offers for prospective TFWs. Like many other TFWs,
he reluctantly paid a series of fees to the agency even though this con-
travenes Ontario employment standards. When I asked him why he
paid so much to the agency, he told me that he found the government
forms too complicated, and his situation was too high stakes for him to
complete the forms by himself. As he explained, "Because to put online
and then fill out the forms for application, I never did myself. And I
found this difficult because I can do the calculation but I'm scared. If
I make a mistake on my file I lose $1,000. So I give $500 to the [agency
name] or lose $1,000 to government" (TFW15, male retail worker from
India, working in Alberta, NOC 6611, skill level D; later working as a
retail manager, NOC 0621, skill level A).[18]

In agency theory, this information asymmetry and its deleterious
effects on the TFWs are, again, unsurprising. The TFWs hire the employment agency or immigration consultant because of their expertise,
which means that the TFWs are likely to be unable to accurately gauge
whether it is making decisions that are advantageous, legal, and ethical.
The TFWs may have specialized expertise in their jobs, but they are
typically not experienced in legal matters, and many lack post-secondary
education or advanced training in English or French. The TFWs cannot
adequately verify the agent's abilities or skills at the time of hiring,
known as adverse selection in agency theory terms. Moreover, TFWs are
also at risk of moral hazard; they cannot guarantee that the agent will
put forth the agreed-upon effort.

TFWs and Agents: Different Attitudes toward Risk?

Agency theory assumes that agents are more risk adverse than principals,
the thinking being that the agent's business is less diversified than the
principal's. Rationally, therefore, agents should avoid any behaviours
that would threaten the viability of their business, including violating

any regulations or offering poor service to their clients. Principals, in contrast, are assumed to be risk neutral because their businesses are more diversified.[19] We can thus infer that employment agencies and immigration consultants should behave cautiously and avoid unnecessary risks to the sustainability of their business (e.g., by avoiding errors or violating any regulations).

However, employment agencies and immigration consultants in Canada experience very few risks. As noted by several scholars, employment agencies are rarely prosecuted for contravening licensing regulations or employment standards.[20] Some provinces (i.e., British Columbia, Alberta, Saskatchewan, Manitoba, Quebec, Nova Scotia) require anyone who recruits TFWs to be licensed. Employment agencies in Ontario and Manitoba are not permitted to charge TFWs or employers for immigration advice because this can only be provided by licensed immigration consultants or immigration lawyers. According to the Canadian government:

> No person shall knowingly, directly or indirectly, represent or advise a person for consideration [unless] they are (a) a lawyer who is a member in good standing of a law society of a province or a notary who is a member in good standing of the Chambre des notaires du Québec; (b) any other member in good standing of a law society of a province or the Chambre des notaires du Québec, including a paralegal; or (c) a member in good standing of the College [of Immigration and Citizenship Consultants], as defined in section 2 of the College of Immigration and Citizenship Consultants Act.[21]

The College has a licensing exam and, before writing it, candidates must have graduated from an accredited program (e.g., Queen's University). The College facilitates an internal complaints process and it shares information with the RCMP and the Canada Border Services Agency.

In practice, this means that advice on how to fill out the LMIA or permanent residency paperwork can be offered by employment agencies and immigration consultants for "free," but this cost is then subsumed within the other fees that they charge. Indeed, as noted above, ongoing reports suggest that many TFWs are charged exorbitant fees[22] to come to Canada for work (as discussed in chapter 1).

A second reason why employment agencies and immigration consultants bear few risks is that there is little chance that they will run out of TFWs, even if they provide poor service. With a worldwide market for labour and a sustained demand from potential labour market entrants, these agents face few reputational risks if they provide TFWs with bad advice. In essence, the TFWs are easily replaceable. Indeed, some TFWs have no choice except to use a specific agency when they are looking for work in Canada. Most of the larger employment agencies have established relationships with a range of employers that include restaurant chains, the agricultural sector, and retail stores in Canada. The TFWs need to choose their agencies carefully, because this choice will determine if a particular employer will even consider hiring them. As a high-wage restaurant worker from the Philippines explained to me:

> A friend of mine who also used to work with [restaurant chain], so she gave me the information and she said that, oh, you have to apply to this recruitment agency because it's faster compared to the other one. The other agency is top notch when acquiring Filipinos to be deployed in Canada for [other restaurant chain]. However, that agency so to speak focused on high-profile candidates such as store managers or assistant managers. So I thought of, you know, this will be quite lengthy for me to wait for them. So I tried to go to the new one, who deploy Filipino workers from [restaurant chain], with previous [restaurant chain] experience to Canada. (TFW58, male food services supervisor from the Philippines, working in Newfoundland as a restaurant worker; NOC 6311, skill level B)

There is some competition between agencies to work with employers in Canada, but in many cases each agency has an exclusive contract with a specific employer to hire all that employer's workers from a particular country. This contract means that any potential TFW who would like to work for a particular company must apply through that specific agency. Agricultural workers have even less choice about which agency they will use because most employers from the agricultural sector use a very small handful of liaison agencies (e.g., FARMS, FERME).[23]

The situation is further complicated by the fact that these agencies are not necessarily at arm's length from the employers they are representing. Several TFWs explained to me that the agent or immigration consultant they were told they must use was a friend, relative, or employee at their prospective place of employment. For example, one TFW from the Philippines, who worked as a bottle sorter in Alberta, paid $5,500 to an agent who was also his boss's friend and accountant. In this case, the agent was unlicensed. When the TFW was informed by the government that his paperwork would not be approved, he stopped working with her, which angered the employer (TFW12, male bottle sorter from the Philippines, working in Alberta and then British Columbia; NOC 9619, skill level D).²⁴ In this case, the TFW was unable to choose whether or not he would engage in a principal-agent relationship with this employment agency. At first, he was unable to assess the likelihood that the agent had adequate expertise or would put forth sufficient effort in assisting him. Once the outcome of the relationship became clearer, he terminated it. However, there were no lasting adverse consequences for the agent or the employer; they would simply find another TFW to replace him.

TFWs may have sought the services of an agent to balance the disproportionate power of their future employers, but in fact they entered into a potentially fraught relationship with its own complexities. Interestingly, the employers were also frequently dissatisfied with the quality of the services provided by the agents, albeit for somewhat different reasons.

Problems with Agencies and Immigration Consultants, from Employers' Point of View

The employers who used employment agencies and immigration consultants seemed to pay less per TFW than what the workers were being charged directly. Whereas most TFWs paid about $5,000 to their agencies, the costs for each employer ranged from $500 to $8,000, with the average being about $1,000 to recruit a worker (via an agency) and $2,000 to fill out the relevant LMIA paperwork (by an immigration consultant). These fees did not include other costs such as the $1,000 federal LMIA application fee, plane fare, or health insurance for the first three months of the TFW's employment. Most likely, the business model for legitimate charges was based on volume; many employers paying smaller fees to the agencies would be less risky (and more profitable) than larger fees paid illegally by a smaller number of TFWs.

Overall, the employers tended to view the agencies as expensive. In a typical exchange, I asked one employer who had hired a nanny through an agency how much the agency had charged her. She told me, "Oh, I think it was $1,000. Is that pretty average? It seemed high. Well, $1,000 is a lot of money" (MAN27, female employer of an in-home caregiver in Ontario). As with many things, the costs were somewhat higher in Toronto. I spoke to an immigration consultant with intimate knowledge of the costs of hiring TFWs, who told me, "The program is so expensive now, right, and there's all this work involved with the advertising, I mean, I would say it ranges anywhere from, I mean there's some bottom feeders out there, but I would say anywhere between $1,700 to $3,000 in the Toronto area. I would say it's definitely higher in the Toronto area and probably lower in the Western provinces because people don't, I mean, would like to charge more here, but people just wouldn't pay for it" (MAN26, female immigration consultant in British Columbia).

Agents and Employers Have Different Goals

Employers (i.e., principals) have somewhat different goals than the employment agencies and immigration consultants (i.e., agents) that they hire. Whereas both parties are seeking to place a TFW at a company, the agent is more concerned with volume and the employer is more concerned with the quality of the TFWs. That is, the business model of the employment agencies and immigration consultants requires that a certain number of TFWs be placed each year, while each employer who uses these services is more concerned with receiving TFWs with the requisite skills and qualifications, who are motivated to work hard, and who will stay at the employer for the duration of their contracts.

The employers who used recruitment agencies or immigration consultants were often unimpressed with the quality of service that they received, to the extent that many managers who spoke with me had initially used an agency but then discontinued doing so. Quite frequently, there was a sense that the agencies did not add much value. One employer I spoke with had hired a series of nannies but found the experiences disappointing: "I did try with an agency, and they sent me someone, but it was, I could already see the mess that sometimes agencies create. And I know a lot of great agents, but I'm having a hard time with understanding their value when they do the same thing as I do" (MAN28, female employer of an in-home caregiver in Ontario). This employer listed the various expenses involved in hiring an in-home caregiver, and then told me, "And guess what? That nanny arrives, she can leave you right away ... They say, 'Oh yeah, no problem. You have three kids. Yeah, I'll take the job. I'll take the job.' Guess what? They arrive. They don't want to work with three kids. They only want to work with one kid. So they quit."[25] Turnover was especially frustrating for employers whose primary reason for seeking a TFW was to have an employee who would stay as long as they were needed. Although there is a general perception that TFWs are hired because they are cheaper, many employers prioritize other factors, such as availability and low turnover.[26] However, the agencies could only facilitate the hiring process; they could not guarantee any outcomes.

According to agency theory, an outcome-based contract is more efficient, but it transfers more risk to the agent, who is already risk adverse. In other words, the employers would likely be more satisfied with the agents if they could insert a clause into their contracts that the employment agencies or immigration consultants would only be paid (or avoid paying a penalty) if the employer deemed the TFW to be suitable after a set probationary period. Agents, of course, would resist an outcome-based contract because they would incur additional costs if they needed to accurately gauge TFWs' qualifications and suitability, for how they would perform at the employer's workplace. Agents' expertise lies in navigating the TFW program, not in assessing language proficiency, specialized job skills, or the "soft" skills or intercultural competencies that are necessary for a successful career in Canada.

Indeed, many employers found that employment agencies did an inadequate job of prescreening TFWs' language skills and suitability for the job. Because the service and the associated fees were fairly expensive, the employers felt that the quality of the workers provided should be higher – and once the TFW had begun work there was no recourse to the agent. As one manager in the tourism and hospitality industry in British Columbia explained to me:

> The agency did not make a fair evaluation of their language skills. They were culturally not prepared. The Mexicans were, it was like a haphazard approach. I think they advertised for them and then people applied for the positions ... It seemed like the agencies were just trying to fill our quota ... In Mexico we paid a Mexican agent who got paid by the placement ... So once they signed the contract, there was one part paid, in my memory it's roughly like this, and then they got paid the full final price on arrival in [city], and they got paid that whether or not the person was successful here or no. (MANI3, male tourism and hospitality employer in British Columbia)

This manager then stopped recruiting TFWs from Mexico and began recruiting TFWs from the Philippines, but without using an agency. When this became unworkable because of changes to how the federal government was administering the TFW program (e.g., limits on the percentage of the employees at the company that could be TFWs), he turned to an agency that hired Canadian employees. He found that with these employees, there was still high turnover. As he explained, "The agency that we used, who they were, they used to do TFW, and then when the TFW for hospitality was shut down, they had to find another business. The agency then switched to the model of trying to get eastern young people to come to the west for a season of employment. And we just found that their people didn't stay very long." In this case, the employer was not able to find an efficient arrangement with any agent. His goal was to recruit Canadians or TFWs who could perform at a high level, but the agents could not provide these workers reliably at a price that was profitable to them.

Interestingly, this employer's eventual solution was to stop using agencies entirely. Instead, he focused on ensuring that his current employees were satisfied with their jobs. This meant that they would return for several seasons, and they would also recommend the manager and the hotel to their friends. He told me that "the biggest way that we get Canadian workers to work for us is because their friends were here and they had a really good time in [city], and they tell their friends in the east, you know, we had a great time in [city]. Come to [city]. That's actually more successful than advertising, interestingly enough, and more successful than using an agency." Although these employees' and employer's goals were different (i.e., an enjoyable workplace vs. high-performing employees with strong language skills), they were more closely aligned than the goals of the employer and the agents.

Employers Cannot Verify What Agents Are Doing

As explained above, one of the central principal-agent problems is that the principal has incomplete information about what the agent is actually doing. The agent is hired because of their expertise, and because the principal lacks this deep knowledge they cannot easily verify whether the agent is fulfilling the contract adequately. Earlier, we saw how TFWs often felt as though using an employment agency or immigration consultant was necessary because they lacked English or French skills or a thorough enough understanding of how to navigate the Canadian TFW program – and that this lack of knowledge made it difficult for TFWs to assess whether the agent had the relevant expertise or motivation to provide the necessary assistance. Although employers had better language skills and more familiarity with navigating complex Canadian bureaucracies (e.g., paying taxes), they also frequently lacked confidence in their abilities to comply with all the TFW regulations while completing the requisite paperwork and participating in the ·

program. They thus sometimes faced difficulties that were similar to those of the TFWs.

The main reason why employers continued to use agencies and immigration consultants when hiring TFWs was that they felt that the process had become too complex for them to undertake on their own, even though they had used the program several times. As one owner of a landscaping company explained, "I couldn't begin to fill out the forms. For heaven's sake, I'm a gardener. There are all kinds of traps that you fall into, and you can waste an awful lot of time filling the darn things in. It's better to have somebody else to do it" (MAN25, male landscaping company owner in British Columbia). He hired an immigration consultant to complete what he estimated to be sixty-four pages of application forms.

Because these employers did not have the requisite knowledge to use the TFW program independently, they also lacked the requisite knowledge to verify the quality of the services that the agents provided. Employers who did not (or could not, because of other demands on their time) increase their familiarity with the TFW program over time continued to hire agents to assist with the TFW process. Although I did not encounter an employer who found errors in an agent's work, this may be due to the information asymmetries between the two parties rather than uniformly high levels of agent performance. Employers whose LMIA applications are denied may ascribe this to problems inherent in the TFW program rather than their agents' abilities.

Employers and Agents Have Different Attitudes toward Risk

Although agency theory suggests that principals are more risk adverse than agents, this does not imply that principals necessarily embrace risk. Rather, principals generally strive to transfer as much risk as possible to the agent, even though the agent resists this. In the context of the Canadian TFW program, the most risk-averse employers were those who relied the most heavily on this program for their staffing needs, as well as those who found the costs of using the program to be prohibitive. In these cases, the employers expected the agents to take on more risks associated with the use of the program (e.g., guarantee a positive response to the LMIA application).

In most cases, the employers used agents to reduce their risks of making an error while using the TFW program. For example, one restaurant manager identified the expense as well as the complexity of the process as key considerations, arguing that it was worth protecting his investment by hiring someone to either undertake the entire process or oversee the documents that were prepared. When I asked him if he found the cost of hiring someone to help him with the TFW process to be reasonable, considering what he received, he told me, "Well, there was a time when you didn't do that at all, but now it's absolutely necessary. Well, I'm not sure it's reasonable, because the whole process to bring someone in is probably about $3,000 to $4,000 per person, because you got to pay their airfare and you have to pay the fee there. You have to pay the $1,000 upfront and then you have to pay, if you use some kind of an agency to assist you in the processing in Canada, you know, like document them" (MAN11, male restaurant owner in British Columbia). I asked him if it was worth it, and he replied, "Put it this way. You don't want to submit anything to the federal government that might have an error in it. By error, I mean just an omission, like oops, I forgot that page. So I have another agency here that I have looking over my shoulder before I submit anything. And I have to pay him a fee." In this case, he hired two agents to reduce the risks of using only one.

In some cases, employers sought out agents to assume the risks inherent in their fraudulent use of the program. The employment agencies and immigration consultants are expected to advise employers on how to manage the TFW process so they can recruit TFWs while staying within the parameters of the program. However, they can also provide advice on how to lie convincingly on the federal government paperwork to ensure the employers' request to hire a certain number of TFWs approved. For example, the landscaping company owner explained to me that he had a good relationship with his immigration consultant and had worked with her for several years. He felt that she knew the system very well, and knew exactly what he needed to say on the forms to be successful in obtaining an LMIA. As he said, "We've played the game now often enough and well enough that we seem to be able to get by it, but my immigration consultant keeps shrieking at me because we have these conversations, and I say that this description to these requirements and all of this sort of stuff is insane. And she says, 'Do you want this employee or do you not want this employee?' And I say, 'Oh, well, okay, if you put it that way. Uh-huh. Yeah. Okay, sure'" (MAN25, male landscaping company owner in British Columbia). In his case, the job descriptions for available occupations did not match the job descriptions for the jobs he needed to fill, so his immigration consultant advised him on how to submit job descriptions that would match, even though they did not accurately represent the work that would be done. Using an agent allowed the employer to have plausible deniability that they were misusing the program, should they be audited by the government.

In theory, principals can reduce the risks of using agents by requiring outcome-based contracts in which the payment is provided only once a certain agreed-upon result has been achieved (e.g., a lawsuit is successful), or only using agents for "programmable" tasks – that is, tasks that the principal can specify precisely in advance so as to monitor their completion easily. However, in practice, employers who are using the TFW program cannot use these risk-reduction techniques. First, the outcome (i.e., a TFW who is successful at their job) is too difficult and time-consuming to measure, and I did not see any instances of agents who were willing to defer their compensation or make it contingent upon a TFW's job performance. Second, the employers were not knowledgeable enough about the specific steps that an employment agency or immigration consultant would have to take to specify what they would need to do. Some employers tried to reduce the risks of using agents by involving themselves in the recruitment process, such as by travelling abroad to interview job finalists. However, this tended to be time consuming and expensive and was not a sustainable business practice.

In some cases where the employer sought an agent to assume the risks associated with using the TFW program but did not want to pay the resulting higher costs, this expense was passed on – illegally – to the TFW. One TFW who spoke with me was hired through an agency to work at a fast-food restaurant in British Columbia; the agency charged him $7,000 even though this cost should have been borne by the employer. However, the worker then explained, "We keep in touch while I was at [restaurant] because whenever I need something from the head office I need to go through the agency first ... Like when I decided to process my permanent residence, I can't go directly to the HR or whoever who is the head of [the restaurant], I need to go through the agency and they will talk to the head office at [restaurant]" (TFW25, male restaurant worker from the Philippines, working in British Columbia; NOC 6711, skill level D).[27] He then explained that the restaurant refused to provide him with the documents that he needed for his permanent residence application, and that they required him to continue working with this agency.

In this case, the TFW was resisting an inefficient and expensive process that had been imposed upon him by his employer. The large restaurant chain that employed him had outsourced a basic HR function (i.e., providing documentation of the employment relationship) to a third party, but then required the employee to pay these costs. Hiring a TFW was therefore entirely risk-free for the employer. This process violates British Columbia employment standards, and also represents a stark departure from normal business practice. However, neither the agent nor the employer suffered any adverse consequences.

Fraud

Thus far, the discussion of principal-agent relationships in the context of the Canadian TFW program has centred on legitimate partnerships, i.e., both parties are assumed to have sufficient bargaining power to enter into (and terminate) contracts willingly, and both parties can be said to benefit from the contract. Moreover, these interactions were broadly conducted within the legal framework of the Canadian TFW program as well as Canadian immigration law. However, I came across several instances of fraudulent principal-agent relationships. In other words, one party was deceived or manipulated to engage in economic activity that was not in their best interest.[28]

Recent theoretical research by Pouryousefi and Frooman is useful in explaining how an agency theoretical approach can explain TFWs' and employers' experiences with fraudulent activity.[29] In their analysis of consumer scams, Pouryousefi and Frooman explain how one type of agency problem, adverse selection, is indeed caused by information asymmetries. Their model suggests that agents, with their superior information, aim to appear as though they are promoting the principals' goals, but instead exploit the information asymmetries to carry out the fraud. They further argue that the principal's lack of information, in fact, comprises two separate elements: their inability or failure to observe the agent, and their lack of judgment about any information that they do observe. Taken together, these deficiencies are what leads to the adverse selection, or inadvisable entry, into a contract.

The fraudulent behaviour of the employment agencies or immigration consultants sometimes extends into human trafficking. One owner of a restaurant and wholesale food manufacturer explained that he was approached by agencies asking him to fraudulently "hire" a worker, with the agent paying him (on behalf of a worker) to apply to hire some TFWs through the government. The manager would receive a few thousand dollars per "employee," and each "employee" would then receive the necessary paperwork to live in Canada. There was no expectation that this manager would actually hire these individuals; they would scatter and work elsewhere. He told me:

There's a lot of misuse in the system of bringing foreign workers across, especially in my community. There [are] immigration lawyers. I get a phone call once a week that "Hey, we'll give you $20,000, can you give us an LMIO?"[30] ... I know one person, I don't want to name the person, but in one year he brought I think thirty to forty people from Australia. I don't know, he brought thirty to forty people as cooks from Australia or whatever country. They were originally from India but they all ran away, went to this country and from there thirty to forty of them came here. In one year the guy shut his business down, charged $25,000 each person ... No, I'm not kidding. It's a business for some people (MAN24, male owner of a restaurant and wholesale food manufacturer in British Columbia).

The manager believed that these workers would then work illegally elsewhere, to secure the funds that they needed to repay the loans that they took out to come to Canada. He continued:

These poor people that are in India, some of them just gathered all their money up to put it all on this one guy and then maybe you won't even come here. And sometimes even if you do come here you say you're working for this company but you're not working for that company then you need illegal work somewhere else ... Say if you're saying I came for this pizza store and you're supposed to be legally working there but there is no job there for you. And then you're in Canada; you have to think of something else, then you start doing illegal stuff.

In this case, the employer was able to avoid adverse selection because he knew enough about the legalities of what the agents were suggesting. While the agents may characterize the opportunity as being risk-free and mutually beneficial, the targeted principal (i.e., the employer) was able to interpret the available information accurately and supplement this understanding with additional contextual information about the practices of similar agents. This employer also had a thorough under-standing of the legal risks to his business as well as to his reputation if he were to engage in fraudulent activity. With a reasonably symmetric level of information, he was able to avoid a potentially damaging liaison.

This employer's experiences are in stark contrast to those of many TFWS. One immigration consultant who owned her own agency told me, "We get, just our little agency here, we probably get sometimes ten to fifteen emails, Facebook messages, calls [from people asking], 'I want to work in Canada ... Can you help me?' So the bad ones out there, of course, take advantage of those people, right? Because I could say, 'Sure, I can help you. Send me, I don't know, send me some money and I'll help you'" (MAN26, female immigration consultant in British Columbia). I asked her how much this fee would be, and she told me that it would be approximately $20,000. This agent told me about instances of employers fraudulently "hiring" several nannies per year through the in-home caregiver program, and reminded me of an article in the *Toronto Star* describing seventeen nannies sleeping on the floor of the recruiter's basement because they had all been fraudulently recruited for non-existent employers.[31] As she explained, "Sometimes you really have to wonder [about] the common sense of the people who would pay that much. But they're desperate, right? They want to come."

In this case, the consultant is questioning the judgment of the principals (i.e., the TFWS). However, it is important to note that the TFWS in this case are likely to have incomplete or distorted information from the agent (e.g., they would not be told that they would be sleeping on the agent's floor). They are also likely to lack important contextual information about (a) the legalities of what they are requesting from the agent; (b) their employment alternatives (e.g., legitimate agencies); (c) the track record of the agent and the likelihood of the agent defrauding them; and (d) the effect on their permanent residency status if they are working in Canada without authorization. The TFWS may have some information about the agent, but they may not have enough information to make a decision about whether the agent is trustworthy. Interestingly, the agent described above ascribes the TFWS' willingness to enter into a disadvantageous contract to their desperation. This is certainly a possibility, but the effect of the information asymmetry should not be discounted.

Enduring Problems with Agents: Few Remedies

In other contexts where agency problems pose serious consequences, various remedies are applied. Unfortunately, these remedies may not be practical in the context of agents and TFWS or employers. For example, many corporations address the inherent goal conflicts between CEOS or employees and shareholders by providing the CEO or employees with stock options; the intent is to align the goals of both parties. In practice, this does not always address inherent goal conflicts, because share prices are sensitive to a variety of factors outside a CEO's or an employee's control, but the idea is that CEOs and employees will act in the shareholders' interests if they are also shareholders. However, the interests of agents and TFWs or employers are disparate enough that it is unlikely that they could be joined in a similar fashion.

Similarly, it is sometimes suggested that the market is an effective way to limit the self-interested behaviours of agents.[32] For example, based on an efficient-market hypothesis, corporations with CEOs who act against the interests of their firms would be vulnerable to being eclipsed or bought by competitors. In other words, poor management is said to be unsustainable in the long run. However, market forces alone would not be likely to place adequate pressure on employment agencies or immigration consultants to avoid acting against the interests of TFWs or employers. Accurate information about these agents is scarce and difficult to verify, so the market cannot work efficiently.

The remaining solution is improved regulation. As it stands, employment agencies and immigration consultants face little oversight. The agency owner in British Columbia related examples of individuals fraudulently "hiring" several nannies per year through the in-home caregiver program. She also told me, "We heard of stories [of] agencies where people would pay employers, and they would bring in four nannies a year, right? No questions asked. Nobody asked, looked at this and said, 'Hey, wait a minute. Why is this family hiring all those nannies?' Right? They were charging big amounts" (MAN26, female immigration consultant in British Columbia). In the absence of careful oversight, some agencies are profiting from people who are desperate to work and live in Canada.

I also interviewed an immigration consultant in Ontario who had closed his agency because he did not believe that it was possible to operate ethically. When he first started his business, TFWs were far less regulated, and employers in any province were able to hire him to recruit TFWs and complete the necessary paperwork to obtain an LMIA from the federal government. However, he noted a definite shift in public perception around 2013 after several high-profile scandals spurred changes in how the TFW program was administered. He told me that these changes "got rid of all of the ethical players because all of a sudden now, even if you were doing things 100 per cent ethically and compliantly, even if you had absolutely zero fees to the candidates or even if you offered free immigration services, you were still Public Enemy Number One. There was still absolutely no way to be considered an ethical or compliant player in the eyes of either the public or the government one election to the next, simply because it was such a political issue" (MAN29, male immigration consultant in Ontario).

In his view, the change in public perception and fee structure led to the larger employment agencies leaving the industry. He explained that "as a result, all you get now are the small little illegal operators that are running around charging usually people from their own country who have absolutely no licensing and absolutely no credibility whatsoever, but they're the only ones left. They're the only ones left because everybody else got sick and tired of feeling like the enemy." Based on his experience, this former immigration consultant noted that the absence of legitimate agencies meant that the fraudulent "ghost agencies" had an even larger market for their services, and he believed that these services would continue to operate because they were so profitable. He told me that this was happening because employers now had to "go to these source countries and start looking for individuals themselves. And the second that happens, you get these ghost agents in the home country that are totally unrelated to the equation who are charging $10,000 to $15,000 to $20,000 per person to find them a job." He went on to explain that TFWs now had fewer options when they sought help from legitimate agencies or immigration consultants. They often still felt that they needed to hire someone to help them, because the process was so complicated.

When I asked him how these arrangements were brokered, he told me that most of the ghost agencies relied on extended family or cultural connections. Because the TFWs and employers were working with someone who had community ties, many arrangements were informal and easy to deny, which led to them being difficult to discover or prosecute. As he told me, "The government can't necessarily do much if nobody is declaring that person [on their TFW application paperwork]. Who knows if an employer is working with an unethical agency if there's no real opportunity to do so, if that agency or that person or that cousin or that uncle says no, no, no, I'm just doing it for free?" He explained how very common it was for an existing employee, such as an in-home caregiver, to suggest to her employer that she hire her relative or acquaintance:

She would say, "I know your brother is looking for a caregiver, and I'm really good at the LMIA process, so I'll be able to help you with it. My uncle works for a church or something or is a professional and will do this for us for free, and you don't have to pay anything." It's very hard to understand. I mean, like do you just say no, I don't trust you? And it's usually too late before a lot of these employers realize what's happening because trying to do a favour for somebody is turned into human trafficking.

This consultant admits that he left the industry quite reluctantly. As he said to me, "I was contacted by somebody recently who I worked with seven or eight years ago, who [is] a great employer, a national brand, looking for drivers and mechanics. And I said, 'I'm sorry, I can't do this for you anymore. Unless I'm charging you $20,000 to $30,000 per person, it's not viable. And even with that, there's no guarantee that they're going to arrive. And I don't have anybody ethical that I can refer you to.'"

Conclusion

The evidence from my interviews with TFWs, community support workers, managers, employment agency owners, and immigration consultants suggests that TFWs and employers are frequently disappointed with the cost and quality of the services that these organizations provide. It appears that the use of employment agencies and immigration consultants has become widespread, not because of any particular "value added" (e.g., protections that they offer to workers or employers) but rather as a response to the complexity and uncertainty of the employment approval process. Agencies' fraudulent activities have been well documented outside of Canada,[33] but inside Canada, agencies are frequently charging fees to workers, even though this is prohibited. These fraudulent activities are, of course, problematic, but even the agencies' legal operations seem unsatisfactory to many clients.

Although employers and TFWs were both dissatisfied with many of their interactions with agents, the employers were taking on less risk when using an agent than the TFWs. For the most part, they had several alternatives if the agent that they had hired failed to deliver; they could seek non-TFW employees, they could use other agents, and they generally had more financial resources than the TFWs did. They were also less vulnerable to information asymmetries because they had a better understanding of the Canadian legal environment as well as the typical costs involved in using an agent. In contrast, the TFWs had little information about what the agents could provide, this information was frequently distorted, and they had difficulty interpreting the information that was available. Low-wage TFWs and in-home caregivers were particularly vulnerable in this regard.

Moreover, the growth of employment agencies and immigration consultants is problematic in other ways. Using an intermediary may unintentionally discourage TFWs from engaging directly with the government. If problems arise with their employment contract (as discussed in chapter 1), they may be more reluctant to seek advice from the government because this would be their first time doing so. As discussed above, several TFWs who spoke with me sought assistance from their agencies when their employer mistreated them or when they wanted to find a new employer; however, when their agencies minimized the TFWs' concerns, they did not pursue the matter any further. If these workers had completed their paperwork themselves, they may have developed more confidence in dealing with the federal government and they may have felt more comfortable reporting unsafe or unfair working conditions.

Employers that rely too much on employment agencies are choosing an expedient option, but they are also missing an opportunity to develop strategic HR skills. Especially in the low-wage and high-wage streams, employers that hire TFWs should be developing long-term plans for how to address their need for labour. On the LMIA form itself, employers that are requesting permission to hire low-wage or high-wage TFWs must list several new ways that they are trying to recruit qualified workers who are Canadian or permanent residents (e.g., job fairs, internships, partnerships with unions or colleges). When an immigration consultant fills out this form on behalf of an employer, the employer loses the opportunity to seriously contemplate how to sustainably address their labour shortage. Moreover, one of the ways in which the employer can demonstrate to the federal government that they are seeking to hire Canadians or permanent residents is by explaining that they intend to help the TFWs that they employ apply for permanent residency. The immigration consultants who help employers to complete these forms benefit directly when they suggest this option because they can then provide assistance about this process (for a fee).

Employers and TFWs hire agents to reduce the risks associated with information asymmetries, but unfortunately the resultant business relationships remain complex. Although the transaction is short-term, there are high stakes – especially for TFWs, who have few resources and few alternatives.

Family

Social Capital under Strain

Unfortunately, the problems temporary foreign workers (TFWs) face are not limited to those they experience in their workplace or at the hands of their agents. TFWs' personal lives are frequently upended by moving away from their families; although seeking work in Canada is often financially necessary, it comes at the cost of family relationships. Moreover, TFWs who are separated from their existing social networks are more vulnerable to oppressive or exploitative work arrangements because they have less access to information and support.

In this chapter, I define social capital and explain its role in accessing resources. I then identify four typical family situations for TFWs in Canada: living apart from their families, bringing their families with them to Canada, creating new family structures in Canada, and coming to Canada to work for a relative. For each situation, I explain how these TFWs' social capital is affected by their transition to Canada, and how the resultant varying levels of social capital affect the success of their transition. I also describe the contrasting experiences of a non-TFW who came to Canada with an open work permit, and I explain how she was able to maintain her supportive social network.

Social Capital

Social capital refers to the idea that social ties can have positive outcomes for individuals and communities. It is fundamental to many areas of inquiry in organizational behaviour, but the construct of social capital has much earlier roots in sociology. Bourdieu defines social capital as "the aggregate of the actual or potential resources which are linked to possession of a durable network of more or less institutionalized relationships of mutual acquaintance and recognition."[1] A key aspect of social capital is that it comprises two separate elements; the social relationships themselves, which enable individuals to access resources through others, and the amount and quality of these resources.

The social exchange that is facilitated by social capital differs significantly from economic transactions; first, the currency with which obligations are repaid may be different from that with which they were incurred in the first place, and it may be as intangible as granting approval or allegiance. Second, the timing of the repayment is unspecified. For example, one person might do a small favour for a neighbour (e.g., collecting mail while they are away), and the neighbour might repay it with a different favour (e.g., a gift of zucchini from their garden later in the summer). Indeed, exchanges where one individual specifies the way or timeline to reciprocate a favour or other obligation are economic rather than social exchanges. Although both economic and social exchanges are useful, there are clear advantages for individuals who have high levels of social capital, defined both in terms of their large number of social ties to others as well as the high quality of resources they can access. Among other advantages, social capital helps individuals find jobs and it influences their compensation and career success.[2]

When evaluating an individual's social capital, it is important to distinguish between their "strong" and "weak" ties. The strength of a tie is based on a combination of the amount of time, the emotional intensity, the intimacy (e.g., mutual confiding), and the reciprocal services that characterize the tie.[3] Strong ties are important because they provide network members with social support and mutual assistance. However, weak ties are also important. Weak ties bridge different social networks, and thus they are more likely to provide social network members with useful yet difficult-to-access information (e.g., job leads). An individual's weak ties (e.g., acquaintances) are privy to knowledge that their strong ties (e.g., family members) do not have. Individuals with a mix of strong and weak ties therefore have the social and instrumental support they need to thrive.

Like any form of capital, social capital requires investment; individuals who seek to benefit from the resources of their network must put forth effort in developing and maintaining these relationships or social ties.[4] As social exchanges continue between individuals, the relationships are strengthened and trust develops further. I explain below how TFWs with various family situations face different challenges in maintaining and building both strong and weak ties, and how these frayed or missing ties pose varying difficulties for them as they try to work safely in Canada.

TFWs Who Live Apart from Their Families

Most TFWs who come to Canada do so without their families. TFWs in the Seasonal Agricultural Worker Program (SAWP), for example, are prohibited from bringing their spouses or dependents with them. TFWs in the low-wage program, in contrast, are able to bring their families but must demonstrate that they are able to support them financially even if their spouse may not be eligible to work in Canada. This is difficult to demonstrate, given the low wages. In cases where a foreign government agency has a role in selecting workers for the Canadian TFW program (e.g., in the SAWP program), some countries prefer to approve the applications of TFWs who have spouses and children. The presence of a family is taken as evidence that workers are highly motivated to work and that they will return to their country of origin when they have completed their contracts.[5] What emerges, therefore, is the common but heart-wrenching scenario where parents move to Canada to support their families, knowing they will be separated from them for very long periods of time.

Not surprisingly, this extended involuntary separation causes hardships for the TFWs' children. For example, the children of Mexican SAWP workers have been shown to be more likely to feel abandoned by or estranged from their fathers, have more health and behavioural problems, and perform poorly in school.[6] These workers' wives report feeling overwhelmed by the added responsibilities that they take on when their spouses are absent. A similar phenomenon has been identified among the children of Filipina live-in caregivers.[7] When their mothers move to Canada to work, they are usually left in the care of grandparents or other extended family members for months if not years, waiting until their mothers are eligible for Canadian citizenship and they can be reunited.

Of course, the remittances that TFWs send back home are crucial for their families' survival.[8] In many of their home countries, unemployment is high, wages are low,[9] and education and social services are funded privately rather than through taxes. The remittances are therefore necessary to pay for basic needs such as shelter, food, clothing, and medical care as well as primary and secondary school.[10] In some cases, the remittances that Mexican SAWP workers send to their families help them to increase the profitability of their own farms and diversify their income streams (e.g., by enabling the family to start a business).[11] Family separation is often seen as a necessary hardship for families seeking economic stability.

Although TFWs necessarily prioritize economic stability, the process by which they earn it frequently damages TFWs' previously strong ties to their families and local communities. The TFWs are necessarily spending less time with their families, and it is difficult for them to maintain an emotional connection even with daily telephone and Skype or Zoom calls. The reciprocity of their relationships diminishes, because one spouse is tasked with providing financially for the family while the family cannot provide immediate intangible support. Most damagingly, the intimacy (i.e., mutual confiding) – and therefore the trust – in their relationships is ruptured, thereby straining the formerly strong ties.

A construction worker from the Philippines explained his experiences to me. When we met, he had just begun working additional shifts as a security guard at the construction site where he was employed so he could send more money home for his wife and three children. Money was tight, because his wife was paralyzed and had difficulty working. Sadly, one of his children had died in 2012, before he came to Canada. He had trained as an engineer, and when I asked him why he would come to Canada to work as a labourer instead of working as an engineer in the Philippines, he told me, "My wife insisted me to come here because of the salary. And she said if you are working in the Philippines you will not earn enough money to send me back home. So when we computed it and talked to each other, yes, you're right. I finally said say yes to her and okay I will go for two years and they will rehire me another two years and I will come back home. I told her that. I really miss my family" (TFW16, male construction worker and security guard from the Philippines, working in Alberta; NOC 7611, skill level D).

I asked him if it was easy to talk with his wife about this, and if she understood how much he missed being away from her. "It's hard for her to understand," he said. "I didn't tell her all my experiences yet, because I don't want her to get disappointed. But maybe when I come home and we have a bonding together she will understand it. I'm beginning to cry ... Sorry for that." I told him not to apologize, and I apologized for bringing up a sad topic. He then said, "I can bear the hardship but I can't bear what's going on in the back of her mind." In his case, he hoped to return to the Philippines as soon as possible, although his employer was withholding some of the funds for his return plane ticket. He worried about being able to support his family financially in the future, because it would be difficult for him to work as an engineer again; he had been away for so long that his skills and work experience were no longer up to date.

This TFW's formerly strong ties to his family were clearly weakened by the distance and the length of time that he needed to spend away from them. Although, in theory, they could be a source of social support, he was reluctant to confide in them because he did not want to worry them. This lack of mutuality and shared confidences was typical for TFWs, but it risked damaging his marriage as much as the distance and time spent apart from each other. Moreover, his ties to his community in the Philippines were also damaged; he would have difficulty finding a job even if his skills were relevant, because he had not been able to maintain his professional network in the Philippines while working in another field in Canada.

Also troubling was the fact that this TFW also noted, "It's so hard living alone. I don't know anybody." Not only was this TFW dealing with deteriorating strong ties, but he was also unable to develop new weak ties in Canada. Low-wage TFWs like this one typically live in housing that has been arranged by their employers; although one advantage of this arrangement is that the housing is inexpensive, it can also serve to hinder TFWs' integration into the community. Low-wage TFWs may also face income-related barriers to building a robust social network; they may not be able to afford recreational activities or other activities where they could make new acquaintances. TFWs in the SAWP and in-home caregiving programs may face even greater barriers; they typically live on their employers' properties and are even more socially isolated.

TFWs Who Bring Their Families with Them

Depending on the TFW stream, it is not always possible for workers to bring their family members to Canada. For example, as noted above, agricultural workers in the SAWP are not permitted to bring spouses or children with them to Canada. However, high-wage (formerly higher-skill) and in-home (formerly live-in) caregivers are permitted to bring their families with them in some circumstances. The specific guidelines for work permits are detailed under "Types of Work Permits for Your Situation" on the government's website.[12] Some of the key requirements for an open work permit are as follows: High-wage (higher-skill) TFWs can bring their spouses through the Express Entry program, which entitles them to open work permits. This option is only available to spouses of TFWs who are working in occupations with a National Occupational Classification (NOC) skill level of O, A, or B (e.g., a manager, an accountant, or a truck driver). The TFW must also be approved to work in Canada for six months or longer. The open work permit enables the

TFW's spouse to work at any employer in Canada, whereas the TFW's closed permit is linked to a specific employer.

For many years, live-in caregivers were discouraged but not prohibited from bringing spouses or children to Canada. Families were permitted if and only if the visa officer was satisfied that the TFW had enough money to care for and support the family members in Canada and that the employer would allow them to live in the home where the care was provided.[13] When the live-in caregiver program was largely supplanted by the in-home caregiver program in 2019, these rules changed. These workers' spouses could now apply for open work permits (as noted above), and their children became eligible to apply for study permits.[14] Under the new rules, in-home caregivers can no longer be compelled to live in the same home as the person they are caring for and so can find living arrangements for their entire family if need be. While this revised program is available in most Canadian provinces, as of 2020 it is not available in Quebec, which continues to use the earlier program.

Many employers who used the in-home caregiver program told me that they would never hire a nanny who brought their husband or children with them. They only wanted a nanny who would live in their house, even though the recently revised in-home caregiver program guidelines prohibit employers from requiring this. However, I spoke to one in-home caregiver, a single mother from the Philippines, who did bring one of her children with her. Her second son had just been born a few weeks before she received a job offer in Ontario, and she felt that he was too young to leave behind. While her first son stayed in the Philippines with relatives, her baby lived with her pastor's family in a city near where she worked and lived. They would bring her baby to her when they could, so that she could try to bond with him and breastfeed. As she told me, "Here in [city], I took care of an eighty-one-year-old. She is alone in her house. Sometimes the families allow me to bring my child, just to, you know, to breastfeed like two nights. Yeah and my [pastor's] family will pick him up. I just see him every other weekend. Wow. Breastfeeding just last two months though." I asked her how she felt about this arrangement, and she told me that "[it is hard] to leave my baby with somebody and to take care of [an] eighty-one-year-old. There are times when I really can't help but to cry in the night" (TFW02, female in-home caregiver from the Philippines, working in Ontario; NOC Code 4412, skill level C).

In this case, we see how bringing a dependent to Canada did not increase the TFW's social capital. She brought her child with her to bond with him; for her, this was better than leaving him behind but the arrangement was unsatisfying. She was unable to spend much time with her infant, and she could not spend more time with him without jeopardizing her employment. This arrangement continued for one year. She then needed to find child care, which was difficult. As she told me, "I tried also to pay somebody, a parent, who came here and they were willing to take care of my baby also once in a while, so I paid them out of my biweekly $223. I pay them $100 weekly." I asked her to clarify these amounts, because at the time and in this province, this live-in caregiver should have been paid at least $9.25/hour, and her work week should have been no more than forty hours. Based on a forty-hour work week, this TFW was only paid $5.58/hour, unless her pay had been further reduced to pay for her room and board, a violation of the federal TFW guidelines. If she were in fact working more than forty hours per week, which most in-home caregivers report being required to do, then her hourly wage would have been even lower. However, she confirmed: "$100 weekly. And I have to buy the diaper and the milk of my baby. There is really, really nothing left for me." She explained further that her family in the Philippines was upset that she was not sending more money to them, but she simply had nothing to send them. She and her baby relied on donations of food and diapers from her church.

We see, therefore, that this TFW's formerly strong social ties with her family were fraying. Not only was she unable to spend time with them or establish a relationship characterized by emotional connection and mutual assistance (e.g., by performing small favours for each other), she could not even send them much money to help them care for her other children. This TFW was able to establish some new weak ties to community members through her church. However, these social ties were not of a quantity or quality high enough for her to find either a new job that paid her fairly or quality child care that she could afford. Even with a family member with her, she was too isolated to flourish.

TFWs Who Create New Family Structures

It is not unusual for TFWs to form new families while living and working in Canada. I interviewed six workers who had new partners or who were recently married (e.g., TFW06, male farm worker from Bulgaria, working in Ontario; TFW55, male cook from Japan, working in Manitoba). Many of the six had met their spouses online (e.g., TFW12, male bottle sorter from the Philippines, working in Alberta and then British Columbia; TFW13, male baker from Jamaica, working in Alberta; TFW18, male retail worker from Mexico, working in Alberta), but others had met their partners at work (e.g., TFW52, male landscape worker from Mexico, working in Alberta). They were all excited to start a new life with their spouses. It was not surprising to meet so many young couples and newlyweds, considering the ages of the people I interviewed. The median age of TFWs in Canada is between thirty and forty-four,[15] and the average age Canadians marry is thirty for women and thirty-one for men.[16] TFWs who are not already married when they arrive in Canada are likely to want to marry soon.

However, it was difficult for most TFWs to forge close relationships with Canadians. This phenomenon has been well documented in the academic literature on the experiences of TFWs in Canada, and it can be attributed to TFWs' precarious work status, their experiences of discrimination, and their conflicted identities.[17] In essence, it is hard for them to meet Canadians, and Canadians are not always interested in building relationships with them. However, many of the TFWs who spoke to me developed close friendships with roommates and other members of their cultural community. Many of these relationships were facilitated through local churches or mosques, Facebook groups, and loose acquaintanceships with other friends. They were able to cook for each other, celebrate birthdays together, talk about their work, and share information about adapting to Canada. These substitute families, or "fictive kin," have been established as key factors in the success of immigrant communities.[18]

The ability of TFWs to forge new relationships was important to their health and well-being. The experiences of a restaurant worker from Morocco illustrate this. Very fortunately, he developed a close relationship with a local family. He was able to turn to them for help when he lost his job; this was crucial because his shared apartment was only available to him through work. He told me:

This family believed that I am good person, believed that I need help. So they said could you live with us in a place [in location] for free ... my face looks similar to the face of her son and her daughter and her because [it's a] little bit brown. And she like me, this mother I call her momma and my father Mr. [name]. And they have them without nothing and they give me a lot of things. They give me house, they give me food, they give me their patience and they adopted me. I cannot pay them. I don't know how I can pay this family because they keep me from snow, like what we said, and I love them so much. (TFW11, male food services worker from Morocco, working in Alberta; NOC 6711, skill level D)

Unfortunately, these social ties were not strong enough for this TFW to receive assistance from them when he became seriously ill. He had contracted a serious infection because of a very crowded living arrangement before he had met this family. His employer had provided him with a shared apartment, but there were not enough beds for all the workers who lived there, so he slept on the floor for three months. The public health contact tracer who found him informed him of his likely diagnosis when he was living elsewhere, alone. However, when he spoke to a doctor about his condition he learned that it had deteriorated considerably and, after much discussion, he decided to have lung surgery. The problem was that he could not be admitted for the surgery unless he had someone to pick him up from the hospital and take care of him for two weeks while he recovered. Even though the post-operative care would be conducted by a visiting nurse, he did not know anyone willing to help him.

We see how this TFW's prior social ties were not sufficient for his health and well-being. Although he had family living elsewhere in Canada, he could not afford to travel to see them. He therefore never told them that he was sick, because he knew that they could not help him and he did not want to worry them. Moreover, his new social ties were also insufficient; they would have been adequate for helping him to find a new job or living arrangement, but they were not strong enough for him to receive the help that he needed. As with the other TFWs described above, his social network was insufficient, in terms of both strong and weak ties. As a last resort, he posted a flyer at a mosque near the hospital where the surgery would take place. This was not his own mosque; he did not know anyone in that city. However, a man from Turkey saw the flyer and contacted him after asking his landlady for permission to have an overnight guest for two weeks. The TFW then stayed with this stranger while he recovered from surgery. He recovered, but he seemed shaken by his experience.

The social capital in this community was strong; his helper could provide this TFW with assistance and be relatively confident that while this TFW would not be able to repay his favour the other community members would notice his helpfulness and reciprocate in some way in the unspecified future. Although it was fortunate that the TFW was able to access this social network, the fact that he was able to do so speaks more to his luck and his initiative, and to the strength of community in this mosque, rather than his individual social capital or any features of the TFW program.

TFWs Who Come to Canada to Work for a Relative

In addition to providing social support and information or assistance, social capital is also, unfortunately, a source of social control.[19] When many members of a community have overlapping or shared social ties, the actions of any individual within a network are easily surveilled. On the one hand, this close monitoring of people within a social network can prevent rule violations. However, on the other hand, the redundant ties and resultant monitoring can also enforce a code of silence. Less powerful members of a social network may be reluctant to speak out against the conduct of others, lest their closer ties (e.g., family members) face repercussions.

I came across several examples of this situation among TFWs who came to Canada to work for family members. In these cases, they were mistreated by their employer but felt that they had no recourse. They could not complain about their employer/relative to the government because they would risk the disapproval of their extended families in their countries of origin. Nor could they complain to any family members back home because there was too much of a risk that these complaints would be revealed to the relative employing them, resulting in retaliation and further mistreatment.

I spoke to one nurse from the Philippines who had moved to Alberta to work as a nanny for her cousin.[20] Although she would be working for a relative, she assumed that this would be a good chance to earn money and fulfill the requirements for permanent residency. Despite the fact that she was living and working for her extended family, she found the situation very lonely. As she told me, "It was very hard the first few days, the first few months, because you realize that you're far away from home. You're kind of, you know ... the feeling of very lonely, very sad" (TFW33, female in-home caregiver from the Philippines, working in Alberta; NOC 4411, skill level C). In addition to the loneliness, what concerned her was the fact that she was not being paid for her work. This was a complete surprise to her; she and her cousin had discussed the arrangement during the TFW application process. She had assumed that her cousin would treat her fairly, and she thought she would be paid (according to the stipulations of the TFW program). When I asked her if she was surprised that her cousin would avoid paying her, she explained to me, "With my cousin, yes, of course! Because it's different when you're working with a relative. Because you did not expect that! When I was in the Philippines, I was surprised that they didn't tell me that they're not going to pay me. So when I got here, I was kind of very depressed because I didn't expect that I will be receiving allowance only, not the real pay." Her trust in her cousin was misplaced.

In addition to not being paid for her work, she was also charged for her room and board, which violates the guidelines of the TFW program for in-home caregivers. She explained that this meant that she could not afford to buy enough food, which also should have been covered under her room and board. As she told me: "I only received like not even close to $500, like $200, $300 a month. So how can I pay for my bills? How can I buy for my toiletries and some snacks? … And then you're working, like you're basically doing what's on the contract, but you're not getting paid with the actual payment that you're expecting. Yeah, I actually, when I talked to my other friends who are also sponsored by their relatives, they're not being paid, also. Yeah, they're not being paid also. They're being given only allowance."

Because she was arriving from the Philippines, I wondered if she had appropriate clothing for the winter, thinking that her cousin probably took her shopping at a local discount store. When I asked her about this, she told me, "So first I need to buy the needed stuff, like winter jacket, because I didn't have a winter jacket when I arrived in Canada … My cousin did not buy me winter jacket, because it's so expensive. If she's going to buy me, I need to refund, I need to repay her … I don't have. She only gave me spring [coat]. But you know it won't protect me from heavy snow in [city], right?" I asked her how she coped without a winter coat, and she said, "Just sacrifice. I cannot do anything about it."

When I asked her if she had talked to her parents about how she was being treated, she told me that she had spoken to her dad. Unfortunately, this was not very effective. As she explained, "I talked to my dad, and my dad talked to them and they told me that the reason why they sponsored me, because they just wanted to help me to come here in Canada, and paying me with an actual payment is not really the thing that they wanted to do. But then again, at that time when I was applying, they did not give me clear, you know, information about what is the setup, what is my position when I arrive here. So yeah, I was very disappointed when I came here."

Unfortunately, her other relatives found out that this TFW was unhappy in her situation, and described her as being ungrateful for the "help" that the cousin had provided. When the cousin found out, the TFW explained, "She confronted me that she heard from my other relatives that I was complaining. So yeah, she changed, and she sometimes do things in front of me that, like verbal abuse." Because the TFW tried to advocate for her rights, her situation became worse. She found her treatment to be especially demoralizing, because as she put it, "You're not expecting that a relative can do that to you, right?" The TFW guidelines do not prohibit family members from working for each other; however, they do require all employers to follow all regulations regarding pay and working conditions.

In this case, the TFW's existing weak ties (i.e., her extended family) were helpful in finding her a position in Canada as an in-home caregiver. However, as a TFW, her social network was deficient in two ways. First, it could not provide her with sufficient information with which to evaluate the trustworthiness of her relative/employer. Despite her family connection, the ties that connected her to this prospective employer were not strong enough to warn her that the employment relationship would be exploitative. However, because of the family relationship, she erroneously assumed that she had more information than she did. In this regard, there are interesting parallels with the experiences of TFWs who hired agents to find employment, as described in chapter 2. Second, her extant social network could not enforce the contract to which she had agreed. This TFW's strongest and most trusted ties were in the Philippines, and there were no consequences that they could impose on her new employer, who had ample resources of her own.

Moreover, the new (weaker) social ties that she was establishing with her relative/employer were potentially damaging her status within her existing social network; if she were to be portrayed as ungrateful then other network members would become less likely to offer her assistance in the future. And as with many in-home caregivers, it was difficult for her to establish any new social ties with Canadians or even other TFWs; her financial difficulties (and lack of a winter coat) made it challenging for her to meet other people with whom she could develop social relationships. She was dependent on her strong and weak ties, and they failed her.

An Employer's Perspective

Employers were perhaps more instrumental and intentional about using their social networks, which now included TFWs, to recruit more employees. Several managers I spoke with liked the idea of hiring the relatives of their current TFWs. They found that hiring someone through a personal connection was a good way to recruit reliable workers who would get along and support each other. For example, one restaurant owner in New Brunswick started focusing his employee recruitment efforts primarily on recruiting relatives of his current employees. As he told me, "So right now through the Atlantic pilot program, I've got another lady in the pipeline, and she is the niece of one of those original four guys that came over" (MAN07, male restaurant owner in New Brunswick). This manager planned on continuously recruiting additional employees on an as-needed basis by asking his current employees to recommend their relatives. He believed that a further advantage of recruiting relatives of current employees was that he could avoid using an agency.[21]

Whereas using an agency was expensive and potentially risky, for the reasons described in chapter 2, the employer could leverage the fact that his social network included his employees, which now included TFWs who themselves had extensive social ties in their countries of origin. By using this expanded network, the employer thus had access to a large number of potential employees who he deemed to be better qualified and more motivated to work (at minimum wage) in comparison with the local employees in his city. He could collect information about potential employees (e.g., were they reliable and experienced) and he knew that there would also be social pressure on the new (related) employees to stay with their new employer and to perform well. His current TFWs were valuable, therefore, not only in terms of their human capital (i.e., their knowledge, skills, and abilities), which he would pay them for, but also in terms of their social capital, which he could use to recruit and easily manage additional employees.

From the employer's perspective, hiring a relative is a less risky option than hiring a stranger. One manager I spoke with had originally come to Canada as a TFW to work at a convenience store and a gas station. Once he became a Canadian citizen, he opened his own restaurant franchise and immediately hired his cousin's brother-in-law. I asked him how this came to be, and he explained, "Fortunate that my brother-in-law, my cousin's brother-in-law, [was] interested to come to Canada so I gave that letter to him ... they are more reliable and more honest because they know that if they want to get their immigration, if they steal or something, we can fire them and then they will not be a Canadian. So that way is helpful that it is reliable, long term and honest employee you can get" (TFW15, male retail worker from India, working in Alberta, NOC 6611, skill level D; later working as a retail manager, NOC 0621, skill level A).

For this manager, hiring relatives under the TFW program was an ideal arrangement for three reasons. First, he felt that a TFW was a better choice than hiring a recent immigrant, because immigrants were too "demanding." This manager found that the Canadian or immigrating employees that he tried to hire preferred to work at the local Walmart because they would be paid more, they could have a more flexible schedule that took their preferences into account, and they received a 5 per cent discount on merchandise. I asked him if he would ever raise the wages that he paid his employees and he said that this was not a reasonable option because it would reduce his own income.

The second reason he hired relatives was because he discriminated among the people he would consider hiring. He would not hire any students, because he believed that their schedules were not flexible enough. He would occasionally hire a retiree, if he felt that they were energetic enough to work at his gas station and convenience store. He also refused to hire any Indigenous employees, because he had the racist belief that they did not want to work, and specifically because he was once offended when he was once served in a store by an Indigenous employee who gave him his change by placing it on the counter rather than in his hand.

His third reason for hiring a relative was a result of believing it was less risky than trying to hire someone through a more traditional process. When I asked him why he would prefer to hire a relative rather than a regular applicant, he told me that he believed that regular job applicants could easily lie to him about their qualifications and provide fake references. "That's something [like] gambling, because if you hire someone [you know from] ... back home, you have a better chance." He admitted to sometimes trying to hire strangers, but felt "that might be a risk to how they are when they come here ... Over the phone we see that's a normal process, talk over the phone, but we can't check reference[s]." I asked him why not, and he told me, "Because you never know the number they give [you] is correct or not. Maybe they give the number of their uncle, their auntie." Interestingly, this manager preferred not to use an agency, which could presumably check references more thoroughly.[22]

In this case, we see how the employer's own biases and employment practices meant that he needed to find alternative recruitment methods. Because he was providing below-market working conditions and wages, and because he had racist and ageist attitudes toward specific groups of employees, the pool of available employees was small and he was not able to attract applicants who were Canadian or permanent residents. This employer's recruitment method of choice was therefore to seek job applicants with whom he had weak ties, or who were part of his extended social network. The fact that these applicants would be dependent on his continued approval to proceed with their citizenship applications made them even more attractive to him. He was not interested in working with an agency because he would have less control over who the applicants were, and they would not be as dependent on his goodwill to succeed.

In contrast, applicants with familial ties were especially likely to be demographically similar to him, thereby gaining his initial trust. Furthermore, the fact that these potential employees were part of his social network meant that he could use his social ties to gather – and verify – information about them. These potential TFWs would have difficulty keeping information about their qualifications, career aspirations, and job alternatives private, which would reduce their ability to negotiate their working conditions and wages. Moreover, the social network itself could be a mechanism through which this employer would exert control over his employees; they would likely be motivated to honour their contracts with him to avoid repercussions from their strong ties in the social network who might wish to work for this employer in the future.

An Alternative Path

Lest it appear that the experiences of all newcomers to Canada necessarily involve frayed and exploitative relationships with family members, it is useful to consider the experiences of non-TFWs who are working in Canada. I interviewed one worker from Nigeria who came to Canada on an open work permit instead of using the TFW program. When she first came to Canada, she moved in with her father's brother and his family (i.e., her aunt and uncle, and their children). This arrangement suited her relatives because she looked after her niece and nephew in the mornings (e.g., made them breakfast and got them ready for school); this was necessary because her aunt and uncle both had full-time jobs, working shifts. Living with her relatives also suited her because her uncle was able to provide her with ongoing help navigating the complicated Canadian employment paperwork. None of the other TFWs I interviewed lived with relatives, except those who worked for their relatives, because of difficulties finding suitable employment in a specific geographic region.

I asked her why she needed her uncle's help, and she told me that he had helped her at several stages of the application process. When she was first applying to the Canadian government for a work visa, he submitted her forms for her because his internet (in Canada) was better than hers (in Nigeria). Her uncle also helped her to find a job, once her work visa had been approved and she arrived in Canada. Her job search was daunting because she had only a high school education, and she had not worked before. She told me, "My uncle and his wife, they basically went on Kijiji and compiled a list of websites I could go to [and] apply, and instead of applying to a bunch of them, I applied to those who said we can accept people here on work permits and things like that. Ultimately, I got a job from [company, as a receptionist]" (TFW24, female receptionist from Nigeria, working in Ontario; NOC 1414, skill level C). With her uncle's help, she applied for about thirty jobs, and received call-backs from about ten. The job search process available to this worker, as someone with an open work permit rather than someone using the TFW program, is notably different: she was eligible to apply for any job that was posted, and because she was already in Canada it was easier to gather information about her employer before applying. However, the support from her uncle was crucial; with his local understanding of the job market he could provide guidance on what jobs would match her skill set.

Her uncle then helped her to prepare for the job interviews. She laughed as she told me, "I went to a bunch of interviews and they were asking all these questions that I'd never heard before, like what are your weaknesses? For the first one I actually said what my weaknesses are! And my uncle and I had a big laugh over that." Unlike the TFWs who relied on employment agencies, her uncle provided considerable emotional and practical support during her job search. In this regard, her uncle's interests and her own coincided in a way that was unlike what she would have experienced with an agent. While an agent would be motivated to place her at any job as quickly as possible, her uncle took the time to ensure that she found a safe job that would offer her a reasonable amount of stability as well as the potential for career advancement. Moreover, if she decided to quit her job she would not jeopardize her housing, and it would be relatively simple for her to find a new job.

Furthermore, staying with her extended family provided this young woman with more ongoing support than she would have been able to receive from new roommates or her family back home. Indeed, she rarely spoke to her co-workers because they were scheduled so that their breaks did not overlap. When I asked her what it was like to live with her uncle and his family, she told me, "Very nice! I grew up with all of them so it's nice, plus he's my dad's younger brother and a very tight knit family, like family and everything so it's very nice." Her own parents were comfortable with her coming to Canada on her own because they felt that she would be safe, living with her relatives. She told me, "My family back home were not worried about me coming here, because I won't be alone in this big country."[23] The Nigerian worker's living arrangement with her aunt and uncle was the result of a long-standing informal agreement between the members of the extended family to help each other. She explained to me that her uncle was so especially helpful to her because "my dad helped them come to Canada with money and things like that so they spent a lot of their money on the application process. But when it came time to actually come to Canada he didn't have a lot of money for the flight, on top of that they had to have a certificate from the Canadian government." Now that her uncle had established himself in Canada, he was helping his brother by helping his niece. She planned to become a permanent resident and hoped to eventually sponsor her parents to immigrate to Canada under the family reunification program.

This worker's experiences are a stark contrast to those of the TFWs. Unlike the TFWs whose work in Canada ruptured familial social networks in their countries of origin, this worker's arrival in Canada continued an informal agreement or social exchange between her father and his brother, thereby strengthening this relationship. Rather than feeling lonely in her aunt and uncle's house, she felt welcomed because of the central role she was able to play in her niece and nephew's lives. Her new living arrangement was characterized by mutual support and assistance, and was likely to be sustainable over the long term – especially because it was not tied to her employment, which may not be permanent. With the help of her weak social ties, she was able to find a job that matched her interests and qualifications; when these initially weak ties became stronger, she was able to receive (and provide) social support, which had the additional benefits of making her feel safe and included.

Conclusion

In addition to the psychological tolls of employment insecurity and difficult employment relationships, many TFWs suffer additional consequences as a result of their reduced social capital (i.e., diminished strong and weak social ties). These workers have less information about their rights, less social support, and are aware of fewer alternative job option, which means that they are more likely to endure suboptimal employment arrangements. They are thus more likely to rely on formal structures such as employment agencies and immigration consultants.

Workers in the different streams of the TFW program are likely to experience different challenges in maintaining their social capital and in forging new social ties because of the variations in their living arrangements and financial situations. For example, SAWP workers typically live on the farms where they work in housing that is shared with their colleagues. The layout of their housing makes it difficult for them to entertain a visitor comfortably, and many employers have policies that prevent employees from having guests. Many of these farms are in somewhat remote locations, and few workers have access to transportation that could facilitate a visit to a neighbouring community. Moreover, many farms have policies that prevent their employees from leaving the farm property on weekends or evenings. The net result of these circumstances is that SAWP workers have a diminished capacity to build new social ties, and thus must rely on their existing social capital.

Although in-home caregivers frequently work in more urban areas, they face many of the same challenges as SAWP workers, in that their mobility may be limited, which may reduce their opportunities to build and maintain social capital. In particular, many employers prevent in-home caregivers who live on their premises from entertaining guests. In cases where the in-home caregiver is responsible for arranging play dates and other activities for children (e.g., dropping them off and picking them up from school), in-home caregivers may have some opportunities to meet other caregivers. However, their irregular sched-ules may also prevent in-home caregivers from building a social network (e.g., by attending church or community events). Again, in-home care-givers may thus rely primarily on their existing social capital.

Low-wage TFWs do not generally live with their employers, but they do live in housing that has been arranged by their employers so that their rent does not cost more than thirty percent of their wages. These workers therefore frequently live with their co-workers in shared housing. Although these arrangements are sometimes convivial and supportive, they are also at times very crowded and, again, may preclude low-wage TFWs from entertaining guests and building new social ties. Their low wages may also prevent them from taking up hobbies or attending events where they would have the opportunity to broaden their social networks beyond work colleagues. Low-wage TFWs will thus be likely to rely on a social network comprising their existing social ties and their new co-workers.

In contrast, high-wage TFWs have far more autonomy in where they live and how they socialize. Furthermore, they are far more likely to bring their families with them; although this is not necessarily a pana-cea, that would give them greater opportunities for social support and for building and maintaining their broader professional and personal social network. Because they have higher wages than other TFWs, they have more resources available to devote to investing in their social capital by joining local interest groups and participating actively in their communities. They thus face fewer challenges in accessing information than the other TFWs.

There is much to be gained from having TFWs and their families living together whenever possible. Many research studies have demonstrated the effects of work–life conflict – when the energy, time, or behavioural demands of work conflict with an employee's role as a family member.[24] This research has shown that work–life conflict can negatively affect employees' work outcomes (e.g., job satisfaction, organizational commitment, turnover), family outcomes (e.g., marital satisfaction and family satisfaction), and health (e.g., eating and exercise behaviours, stress and depressive symptoms, life satisfaction).[25] However, there is also a growing acknowledgement in the research literature that family life has an enriching effect on workers' well-being, and that families provide social support,[26] which has positive effects on workers' satisfaction[27] and retention (i.e., staying at their current organizations).[28] In some circumstances, it may not be possible for TFWs to bring their families to live with them (e.g., in remote areas or where employer-provided living quarters are necessary but limited), but family unity and interaction should be encouraged.

The role of family members is particularly important because so many TFWs become permanent residents. This trend has held steady since at least 2001, despite the annual fluctuations in the numbers of TFWs in different streams arriving in Canada.[29] There is perhaps a popular perception that TFWs are separated from their families; this perception aligns with other popular beliefs about foreign workers, including the belief that TFWs are in fact temporary. When TFWs bring their families to Canada, this helps them build the necessary social ties that support them in becoming successful and active citizens. While TFWs need to maintain social ties to family members in their countries of origin to maintain their emotional well-being, it is equally important for TFWs to be well connected in their communities in Canada. Socially isolated workers are more likely to be manipulated or mistreated by an employer; even loose social ties are key mechanisms for exchanging information as well as social support.[30] In the absence of trusted peers, TFWs may be more likely to turn to agencies and immigration consultants, with the attendant problems described in chapter 2. Because so many TFWs are socially isolated, governments need to assume that their websites will be the only reliable information source for TFWs. This information must be provided to TFWs in a way that it can be easily understood.

4

International Comparisons

Canada Is Not the Default Choice

The TFWs who come to work in Canada have several options; many of these workers had significant careers either in their countries of origin or elsewhere before they arrived in Canada, even if they were not applying to the high-wage stream. Given the challenges TFWs face in Canada, it is therefore important to first consider how the policies of the Canadian TFW program compare with those of similar programs in other countries. Moreover, TFWs and employers also make these comparisons, and their inferences and conclusions factor into their expectations regarding how TFWs should be treated in Canada.

In this chapter, I explain how the Canadian TFW program compares with similar programs in the United States, Australia, the European Union, Hong Kong, and the United Arab Emirates. I also describe the trade-offs that TFWs make between their various options when deciding whether to pursue work in Canada. Although wages are an important consideration – and are easily quantified – TFWs also value working and living conditions, and their priorities tend to change as their careers progress and more jobs become available to them. Depending on the stream that they are participating in, many TFWs choose Canada because of the possibility of eventually becoming permanent residents; I present data from Immigration, Refugees and Citizenship Canada that explains the likelihood of this occurring for the different types of TFWs. Moreover, many TFWs say that their employers believe they have few employment options, contributing to low expectations regarding how TFWs should be treated.

Canada in Context:
Comparisons with Other Countries

Canadians generally support immigration, partly because they believe that it benefits the Canadian economy.[1] In fact, Canada has the fifth-highest number of foreign-born residents as a share of the total population (21 per cent); higher than Germany (16 per cent), the United States (15 per cent), and the United Kingdom (14 per cent).[2] Canadian immigration policy receives some international praise for its focus on human capital,[3] selecting immigrants based on their individual characteristics rather than preferring specific countries of origin.[4] The current Canadian immigration points system enables newcomers to become permanent residents if they accumulate enough points based on a variety of individual characteristics (e.g., English/French language proficiency, educational achievement). Immigration applicants receive points for a job offer, but this is neither a necessary nor a sufficient condition for a successful application.

Immigrants to Canada tend to integrate relatively well, but immigrants who are former TFWs have even better job outcomes, in earnings and employment rates.[5] Canadians might therefore assume that the TFW program is as internationally respected as the permanent immigration program. However, the Canadian TFW program is, in fact, not so different from guest worker or foreign employment programs in the United States,[6] Australia, and most European countries.[7] Overall, workers' specific rights vary somewhat, but the general regulations are reasonably similar. Although a comprehensive analysis cannot be provided here due to space considerations, I provide an overview below.

These three regions – the United States, Australia, and European Union – were the areas identified most frequently by the TFWs who spoke to me as possible places to work, instead of Canada, but TFWs identified two other countries as useful comparators – Hong Kong and the United Arab Emirates – because many had worked there previously. There are more significant differences between the Canadian TFW program and foreign workers' programs in Asia and the Middle East, where there are fewer protections available to workers. Again, although a comprehensive analysis cannot be provided, I will provide a general overview of the regulations in Hong Kong and the United Arab Emirates after discussing the first three regions.

Even though there is a body of academic literature that examines the experiences of temporary foreign workers in other countries,[8] it does not focus on comparing the Canadian TFW program with those that exist elsewhere. I therefore focus on the official government policies as well as the experiences of the TFWs who spoke to me.

United States

In 2019, the United States issued 766,000 work permits to temporary and seasonal labour migrants, in different programs.[9] The Canadian high-wage TFW program, in particular, is similar to the H-1B visa for people in specialty occupations in the United States in that employers must demonstrate that no suitable domestic applicants are available. The H-1B visa is available to workers with at least a bachelor's degree or other demonstrated competence, and workers must be paid the prevailing wage or the employer's typical wage for similar employees.[10] In this regard, it is somewhat more restrictive than the Canadian high-wage TFW program, which focuses more on wages than a list of specific qualifications.[11] The H-1B visas can be part of a two-step immigration process that leads to many foreign workers eventually becoming American citizens after holding this visa (for up to six years, although extensions are sometimes available).[12] Although the Canadian TFW program does not explicitly include this provision, many TFWs qualify for provincial nominee programs that facilitate their transitions to permanent residency. The H-2B Temporary Non-Agricultural Worker visa is also similar to the Canadian low-wage TFW program, although the H-2B visa is available for only up to three years.[13]

Likewise, the Seasonal Agricultural Worker Program (SAWP) stream of the Canadian TFW program is comparable to the H-2A Temporary Agricultural Worker visa in the United States. Both programs are designed to facilitate seasonal employment for agricultural workers, although there are some differences. TFWs in the SAWP program in Canada must be from specific countries (no such restriction exists in the United States), and they can only enter for up to eight months (up to three years in the United States), but many worker protections are similar (e.g., agents may not charge employees fees, housing must be provided at no cost, cooking and kitchen facilities must be provided).

Australia

The higher-wage and lower-wage streams of the Canadian TFW program are somewhat similar to the Australian Temporary Skill Shortage visa, although the Australian visa is divided into short-term and medium-term programs, instead of the high-wage and low-wage streams offered in Canada.[14] Australia issued about 202,000 temporary and seasonal labour migrant permits between July 2019 and June 2020.[15] As with the Canadian TFW program, Australian employers must demonstrate that no qualified applicants are available and pay the employee no less than the prevailing market wage. However, unlike TFWs in Canada, temporary foreign workers in Australia must have an occupation on a preferred list, which helps to determine if they will be able to stay in Australia for up to two years or four years (with provisions for Hong Kong passport holders to stay up to five years).[16] In Canada, employers are now prohibited from hiring TFWs for jobs in certain occupational codes, depending on the unemployment rate in the relevant region (e.g., security guards in most areas of Alberta).

The SAWP stream of the Canadian TFW program is quite similar to the seasonal worker program stream in Australia, although the list of approved countries (i.e., Timor-Leste, Fiji, Kiribati, Nauru, Papua New Guinea, Samoa, Solomon Islands, Tonga, Tuvalu, and Vanuatu)[17] is different for obvious geographic reasons. Unlike the Canadian SAWP program, which prohibits employers from charging TFWs for transportation and accommodation, Australian employers may charge employees for these costs.[18] The Australian seasonal worker program is significantly smaller than the Canadian SAWP. Australia admitted only 12,200 seasonal workers in 2019.[19]

European Union

The Canadian high-wage TFW program has some similarities with the Blue Card available in the European Union (EU). Like the Canadian higher-wage TFW stream, the Blue Card system focuses on wages, although it requires employees to be paid at least 1.5 times the national average wage (rather than requiring a wage above the median wage rate in the relevant region).[20] However, the Blue Card work permit lasts longer (between one and four years), and applicants are only bound to their employer for the first two years (although exceptions may be made depending partly on which EU country the worker lives in).[21]

The EU regulations for seasonal workers are quite different than those for the SAWP stream of the Canadian TFW program. Workers from seventy-nine non-EU states are eligible to come to the EU (e.g., Algeria, Morocco, Russia), and there are further agreements between some non-EU states and individual EU countries.[22] Seasonal work can include a variety of industries, including agricultural work and tourism, and seasonal workers are allowed to change their employer once[23] during their work term. Different EU countries apply further restrictions; for example, France limits workers' stays to a maximum of six months in each rolling twelve-month period,[24] and Portugal issues work permits for only ninety days or less.[25] Because there is significant migration within the EU, the number of work permits issued to temporary and seasonal labour migrants tends to be lower than it is elsewhere (e.g., 29,000 in France;[26] 12,000 in Germany;[27] 4,800 in Italy[28] in 2019).

Hong Kong

Hong Kong has several foreign worker streams. The first stream, the imported workers Supplementary Labour Scheme, is broadly similar to the low-wage stream of the Canadian TFW program; the Hong Kong program allows employers who are having difficulty finding suitable employees locally to recruit workers from elsewhere. The eligibility rules require employers to demonstrate that they are financially capable of employing foreign workers, providing them with suitable accommodation, and guaranteeing their repatriation when the contract (up to twenty-four months) is over.[29] The foreign workers must stay with one employer, and their terms and conditions of work must be comparable to those in the local labour market.[30]

The second program, the General Employment Policy (GEP), offers separate streams for professionals and entrepreneurs. The stream for professionals is intended to fulfill a need similar to that served by the Canadian high-wage TFW program. Hong Kong employers need to show that the employees' academic qualifications or work experience is relevant to the position, pay the employees the prevailing market rate, and show that local workers are not available to fill the position.[31] Foreign employees with this work permit have an initial contract for two years; some employees can apply for a further extension of up to six years. A separate policy applies to professional workers from mainland China.[32]

A third stream, for foreign domestic helpers, is only superficially similar to the Canadian in-home caregiver[33] TFW program. Both programs facilitate the hiring of foreign workers to assist with domestic duties. However, foreign domestic helpers in Hong Kong are paid monthly, and receive at least the prevailing MAW (minimum allowable wage), which is HKD$4,630.[34] Hong Kong has no provisions for a maximum daily or weekly number of hours of work or hours of rest, and although the employees are provided with "suitable" accommodations and "reasonable" privacy, they are required to live with the employers.[35] Employers do not need to demonstrate that they could not hire a local worker before hiring a foreigner.

United Arab Emirates

The United Arab Emirates (UAE) has separate programs for domestic workers and other types of employees. Unlike the Canadian in-home caregiver program, which is limited to employees providing care to a child, a senior, or a person with a disability, the domestic worker program in the UAE applies to a wide variety of occupations, including housemaid, housekeeper, babysitter/nanny, private teacher, private nurse, cook, watchman and security guard, domestic labourer, family chauffeur, parking valet, private agriculture engineer, private sailor, household horse groomer, household falcon caretaker and trainer, and private public relations officer.[36]

Instead of recruiting domestic workers through employment agencies, the UAE uses TAD-BEER centres, whose services are regulated by the Ministry of Human Resources and Emiratisation.[37] Unlike the agencies that operate in Canada, the TAD-BEER centres guarantee visas and provide orientation and training, and sometimes they sponsor the workers directly. As in Canada, the working conditions and remuneration of the domestic workers in the UAE are regulated. However, the working conditions differ considerably: the UAE provides only one day of rest per week; employees work up to twelve hours per day; and there is no provision for overtime pay. However, the domestic workers are entitled to thirty days of paid vacation per year, thirty days of medical leave per year, a round-trip ticket home every two years, and employer-provided job attire.[38]

The UAE also provides work permits for other foreign workers. First, workers obtain a permit from the Ministry of Human Resources and Emiratisation, valid for two months from the date it is issued.[39] Workers can then enter the UAE for employment. At this point, the sponsoring employers complete the remainder of the required paperwork (e.g., medical testing).[40] Limited-term contracts are for specific projects up two years and are not renewable; however, unlimited-term contracts are open-ended and are used more frequently.[41] Part-time contracts are available only to skilled workers, those who have university degrees or who have completed a two- or three-year diploma in a technical or scientific field. None of these contracts stipulate that employers must establish that qualified local workers are not available, nor are there regulations about the wages or working conditions for the foreign workers.

Why Choose Canada?

Like any job seeker, prospective TFWs who are considering employment in Canada will consider a variety of factors when making career decisions, taking into account the characteristics of prospective jobs, organizations, and employment contexts. Indeed, research in human resources management suggests that one of the primary factors that applicants consider is their perceptions of person-organization (P-O) or person-environment (P-E) fit. This research has consistently shown that applicants who feel that they have the same values and norms of the recruiting organization have a greater likelihood of seeking and accepting employment from that organization.[42] Although wages are important, other considerations – such as working conditions – are also important from a fit perspective. Most TFWs initially assessed Canadian employers as providing lower wages than competitors in other countries (e.g., United Arab Emirates), but fairer working conditions.

My research indicates that foreign workers made careful comparisons between countries when they were seeking employment or evaluating their own experiences, and Canada is very rarely the only option for them. Consistent with P-O fit theory, TFWs analyzed their opportunities to find work in a variety of countries, and they considered several related factors, such as wages, exchange rates, and the local cost of living; employment benefits, such as housing, meals, and health insurance; and working conditions. They were concerned about whether they would be paid for all the hours that they would work. Most TFWs felt that they would receive higher set wages in Asia or the Middle East, but also felt that they would need to deal with a variety of suboptimal working conditions, which they preferred to avoid.

Unpaid Overtime

TFWs in Canada described being required to work unpaid overtime in a variety of occupations (as described in chapter 1). However, for TFWs who had previously worked in countries where a similar – or worse – expectation existed, the Canadian expectations and working conditions were considered relatively reasonable. As one restaurant worker explained to me, the nature of the work that he did in Canada or in the Middle East was very similar, but the compensation structure was quite different. He told me, "When it comes to work, it doesn't have much difference. But when it comes to compensation, Canada pays more and the benefits that we have in Canada [are] better than

Dubai. That's why I decided to apply. In Dubai we don't get paid by the hour. They just pay us our salary and we don't get overtime and the health benefits" (TFW25, male fast-food worker from the Philippines, working in British Columbia; NOC 6711, skill level D). In his case, he did not receive the perquisites that many foreign nationals receive (e.g., free accommodation, meals, education) when they work in the Middle East, possibly because of his occupation (i.e., restaurant worker) or his nationality (i.e., from the Philippines). The salary structure and the expectation that he work longer hours than his contract stipulated (without compensation) did not appeal to him.[43]

Reduced work hours appealed to many white-collar workers too, including two TFWs from South Korea, both of whom told me that they preferred the Canadian workplace expectations for unpaid overtime. When they worked in South Korea, they were expected to work exceptionally long hours, without pay. As a computer programmer told me, "The biggest difference is here you don't have [to] work overtime too much. It's very common in Korea, without pay. So [in Canada] after I finish work, I can have my free time" (TFW37, male computer programmer from South Korea, working in Ontario; NOC 2174, skill level B). Sometimes he missed the camaraderie of the long hours with his colleagues, as well as the socializing with his co-workers after work ended for the day, but he appreciated the work–life balance and opportunities to do other things. Similarly, an accountant explained to me that "the working hours they are totally different. Because I used to work until very late in Korea. Sometimes I need[ed] to work until midnight or 2 a.m. Yeah, accountants are tough! Yeah, [in Canada] I can have a balance between work and life" (TFW38, female accountant from Korea, working in Ontario; NOC 1111, skill level A). Compared with the corporate cultures they were accustomed to,[44] they both felt that the expectations in Canada were reasonable.

Occupational Health and Safety

Many TFWs also cited clear differences between occupational health and safety rules and practices in Canada and their previous experiences elsewhere: in training, equipment, leader attitudes, and the work culture or co-worker expectations about the importance of safe behaviour at work. For example, when I asked one restaurant worker about the biggest differences between Canada and India, where he worked before emigrating, he told me, "It's like over here, we had eight safety training sessions on [the] computer and even face to face. So just for safety.

Like this is what you can do; this is what you can't do; this is what you
have to do; what you don't have to do. So where I come from, these
things are, nobody knows, like these things don't even exist. Like there
is no safety training. There is nothing. Like it's like everyone works
at their own risk. If anything happens, oh, I don't know, that's your
problem, that kind of thing" (TFW50, male food services worker from
India, working in Ontario; NOC 6711, skill level D). I asked him why
it was so different, and he replied, "Because there are laws here. That's
why. In my country, who's going to enforce this? There is no law. If
anything, like because a construction company owner, he's a very big
rich guy, so if anything happens to you, who's going to fight him?
Nobody. But here the Labour Board will, no matter how rich you are,
you have accountability to the government. That's why." As in Canada,
all employers in India are legally required to maintain a safe working
environment for their employees,[45] but as this TFW noted, the legislation
may be enforced selectively. In making his comparisons between his
employment opportunities in India and in Canada, the more rigorous
enforcement of safety standards in Canada was a distinguishing factor.
The restaurant industry in Canada has high levels of occupational health
and safety incidents,[46] but this TFW's perception of Canada remained
positive because his referent was his prior experiences in India.

Human Rights

When evaluating the attractiveness of potential jobs in Canada, the
TFWs' assessments were not limited to working conditions. In fact,
they frequently mentioned broader concerns about human rights.
Overall, when assessing their working experiences, TFWs felt that the
employment laws in Canada protected them better than what they were
expecting, based on their prior work experiences elsewhere. For example,
one female landscaper was surprised to find out that she would be paid
the same as her male colleagues. She told me that "when I talked to the
employer, like after a couple of months when we met and everything,
like she was really nice, and I told her: Why did you pay me the same
as them, like as the guys, the other twelve guys or fifteen guys? And she
said: 'Oh, because here in Canada, like we pay the same. Like it doesn't
matter the gender. If it's a girl or a guy, like we have to pay the same'"
(TFW52, female landscape worker from Mexico, working in Alberta; NOC
8612, skill level D). Although Mexico does have pay equity legislation[47]
that is largely similar to that in Canadian provinces, this worker's lived
experience suggested to her that Canadian employers were more likely

than Mexican employers to pay equitably. She therefore viewed Canada as a more desirable place to work.

Furthermore, an in-home caregiver from the Philippines told me that "Canada's really great. One thing I love about this country ... [is that] it's diverse and it kind of like opened me up like with new [ideas, and] I learned a lot of things here, like because back home we're predominantly Catholic, so we're not really into the LGBTQ community. And it's just nice to see like how people are very welcoming with new people like wherever you are and regarding like what's your sexuality. It's very open. It's really nice" (TFW57, female in-home caregiver from the Philippines, living in New Brunswick; NOC 4411, skill level C). The Philippines has few workplace protections for people based on sexual orientation or gender identity, although some limited legal protections exist at the local level or in specific organizations.[48] A trans woman from El Salvador who was working as a TFW in Ontario expressed a similar sentiment in our conversation;[49] she had been advised to seek refugee status in Canada, but instead she was planning to simply immigrate here after having a positive experience working as a TFW, because there are very few protections for LGBTQ employees in El Salvador.[50] Although a new El Salvadorean policy enables people to lodge complaints after they have faced discrimination,[51] many hate crimes continue to be committed against trans people.[52]

Likewise, a hotel front-desk clerk told me that one of the things that he appreciated most about working in Canada was that "we get to keep our own passports. It's not like in the Middle East. I got experience in the Middle East, the employer actually takes the passport,[53] but later on they change it. But here in Canada, no, the employer never did that. And they let us keep our passport, our work permit" (TFW21, male hotel front-desk clerk from the Philippines, working in British Columbia; NOC 6525, skill level C). In this case, this worker was able to move more freely within Canada than he had been able to within the country of his prior employment, and this mobility affected his assessment of his Canadian employer. His experiences are not universal; the experiences of Canadian SAWP employees and in-home caregivers who are confined to their employers' properties are well known and troubling.[54] However, compared with his experiences working in Southwest Asia, this TFW found that his Canadian employer granted him considerable freedom. He thus found Canada, despite the lower wages, a more desirable place to work.

Naturally, many workers also compared Canada negatively with other countries where they had the option of working. The primary issue was the closed work permit, central to the Canadian TFW program, which requires TFWs to stay with the employer that hires them, unless another employer who has permission to hire a foreign worker can be found. TFWs who tried to switch employers found this process to be unreasonably complicated, and they felt tied to their employer for longer than they would have preferred. For example, an agricultural worker from Guatemala told me, "It's better in the US. People who arrive in the US, when you're mistreated working for a company, what do you do? You switch. You don't have to stay with this employer who's a bad employer. But here, you have no choice, you can't switch. Because you're tied to a single employer"[55] (TFW40, male farm worker from Guatemala, working in Ontario; NOC 8431, skill level C). TFWs viewed the Canadian closed TFW work permit as far less attractive than the work permits available in the United States and Europe.

Among the different streams of the TFW program, workers consistently made comparisons between their countries of origin and their available options (including Canada). Issues of occupational health and safety were most salient to workers in the SAWP and low-wage programs, whereas overtime and working conditions were priority considerations for workers in the high-wage and in-home caregiver programs. Human rights concerns were raised most consistently by TFWs who had previously worked in Asia and the Middle East, regardless of stream. It is important to note that many TFWs who spoke to me did not feel as though their rights were consistently or fully protected in Canada (as described in chapter 1); however, they frequently felt that their rights were more protected in Canada than they had been in other countries where they had worked previously.

Ongoing Comparisons

Moreover, TFWs' decisions regarding which countries to work in were not unitary. Differentiation-consolidation theory (DCT) states that job applicants may form preliminary perceptions of prospective employers early on in their job search but typically revise these perceptions as they gather more information.[56] DCT suggests that decision makers positively or negatively adjust and update preferences and attitudes toward individual alternatives as they gather more information over time. This process unfolded for TFWs as their careers progressed; early in their careers they would often prioritize one set of criteria (e.g., wages, availability of hours, exchange rates), but then begin to prioritize other criteria, such as working conditions, as they gained more experience. Of course, as they gained more work experience, they also had a broader set of job offers to choose from. For many TFWs, decisions that were initially fairly straightforward early in their careers became more complex over time.

Some of the most appealing aspects of Canadian workplace culture were intangible. Several TFWs noted that they were pleasantly surprised at how respectfully they were treated by their Canadian supervisors and colleagues. For example, the hotel front-desk clerk described above told me, "I'm comfortable telling my boss, expressing what I think should be done or not, reporting something. This is the one thing I love [about] working here … it's easy to say something or to express something. Compared to my previous experiences, especially in Bahrain, I consider myself lucky. I get to work with colleagues who recognize me for what I can contribute as far as my experience and knowledge [are] concerned" (TFW21, male hotel front-desk clerk from the Philippines, working in British Columbia; NOC 6525, skill level C). For this worker, deciding to stay in Canada was part of an iterative process as he continually added new information about his available options and the quality of these options to his decision process. Early in his career, his options were more limited and the available wages were the primary consideration. Because many Canadian tourism companies prefer to recruit experienced employees from the Middle East, he began to have more options as his career progressed. However, as time went on, salary became less important to him than the working conditions and, especially, the characteristics of the work that he would perform. In Canada, he felt that he had more autonomy and more respect from his co-workers, and weighted this consideration as more important than the salary associated with this job.

The experiences of an engineer who spoke to me were particularly instructive. He was born in India, but immediately found that there were few opportunities for him there commensurate with his education and aspirations. He then worked at several jobs in the Middle East, which he chose because the wages were very high. However, this TFW felt that his expertise was not appreciated there. Initially, he found that his financial compensation was sufficiently motivating, but this waned over time and he eventually sought opportunities where he would be paid well and have an opportunity for higher job satisfaction. His job search took him to the United States. In Texas, he found a job where not only was he reasonably well compensated, but his expertise was also respected; this respect had become more important to him. He initially found the work interesting and enjoyable. However, he ultimately found that the scope of his duties was uncomfortably narrow, and he applied to work in Newfoundland as a TFW.

Even though he had significant previous work experience as a senior process engineer, he was initially hired only as a process engineer. However, as he explained, "as soon as they realized that they can utilize my experience ... now they made me a team leader, and like I'm holding seven, eight people working under me, and they are directly reporting [to me], and the work what I wanted to do, they keep on doing it. I'm monitoring or observing their work and all those things ... Like I came in one-third of my paycheque, but I don't have any regret about that" (TFW59, male refinery process engineer from India, working in Newfoundland; NOC 2134, skill level A). At this point in his career, this TFW felt that the opportunity to take on a leadership position was worth a 66 per cent cut in pay. Interestingly, the substantial change in his job description was in violation of the TFW guidelines even though it benefited the employee; the company should have recruited for the more senior position. The fact that they could demonstrate that no Canadians could be recruited for the more junior position was misleading; if they had advertised the actual working conditions and job responsibilities, they may then have received more Canadian applicants and not needed to hire a TFW.

A Potential Path to Permanent Residency

Aside from the considerations related to the job itself, many of the TFWs who spoke to me were motivated to come to Canada because it offered them the possibility of becoming a permanent resident and, eventually, a Canadian citizen. Depending on a variety of personal factors (e.g., level of education, country of origin, occupation), this option was less likely to be available to them in other countries. Indeed, when I asked the restaurant worker in British Columbia (introduced above) why he chose to come to Canada instead of remaining in Dubai, where he had been working for several years, he told me that "one of the reasons why is that I can be a permanent resident here in Canada, but in Dubai there are no ways to become permanent. You can renew the contract for as long as you want but there is no way you can become a permanent resident" (TFW25, male fast-food restaurant worker from the Philippines, working in British Columbia; NOC 6711, skill level D). Any Canadian employer that is recruiting TFWs in the low-wage, high-wage, or in-home caregiver streams can offer something that employers in many other countries cannot: a tentative path to citizenship.

Most TFWs were willing to accept a demotion to a lower paying or less interesting job in Canada if it meant that they would have the chance to eventually become a permanent resident. For many TFWs, this was a careful decision that balanced immediate hardship against potential prosperity. As one fast-food restaurant worker from Bangladesh told me, "This is a job I took to essentially get my foot in the door and start to get my citizenship. To be honest, I'll be honest with you, I don't say this to my owner but I'm saying it to you, I'm here for a citizenship. I'm not here to work [at company name]. I mean, not here. I want to work. I want to work where my strengths are. I don't want to work here. I want to work in a corporate office. I want to work in a bank. I want to work in a marketing firm" (TFW44, male food services worker from Bangladesh, working in Ontario; NOC Code 6711, skill level D). Like many TFWs, given his qualifications he was underemployed for his position. Employers are reluctant to hire workers they consider overqualified, because they are concerned that they will be bored or will quit as soon as a more attractive position becomes available to them. However, many employers will make exceptions for overqualified TFWs, because they expect that they will remain in the job for the duration of their contracts, as part of their efforts to gain permanent residency.

The caregivers have the clearest path to permanent residency, because of the unique nature of this TFW stream. In-home caregivers are now pre-screened for eligibility for permanent residency and then must complete twenty-four months of work as an in-home caregiver – after which they may apply for permanent residency. I spoke to several former nurses who had worked in hospitals in the Philippines before coming to Canada to work as caregivers. I asked one of these workers what had prompted her to quit her job – which was reasonably well paid and had good working conditions – to move to Canada for a far less desirable job. She told me, "When I came here, when I was told that I was only receiving this kind of money, I was very surprised because I can earn that in the Philippines. So I said what's the use of coming here if I'm only earning this much? So I said, the purpose is just to get the papers. You know, getting the permanent resident card, that's it. Yeah, that's all that's the purpose of coming here. It's not really about the job. It's about the dream of being a resident of Canada" (TFW33, female in-home caregiver from the Philippines, working in Ontario and Alberta; NOC 4411, skill level C). She hoped to return to nursing eventually, but in the meantime it was worth it to her to work as a nanny if it meant that she and her children could eventually become permanent residents in Canada.

Unfortunately, the prospect of permanent residency meant that many TFWs were even more vulnerable to mistreatment, because they would endure a lot to become permanent residents. I spoke to TFWs who had experienced mistreatment from co-workers or managers yet were very reluctant to complain because they were concerned that an official complaint would cause their application for permanent residency to be denied. As one cook from Morocco told me:

> It happen[ed] to me that I faced racism … I complained. I complained to the kitchen manager first, then [the] general manager. No action was taken. And then I complained to the employer, the last one is the employer. And then nothing changes. And I had to talk to my immigration official. And the immigration official guide[d] me to where I [was] supposed to complain. I fill out the forms. I explain everything, especially racism, religious racism, colour racism, the hard time in workplace. I explain everything. But last minute I changed my mind … I thought if I raised that form of, if I raise an official grievance or an official complaint, to be honest with you, I was worried about my future here in Canada. They may say, I don't know, but I was thinking that I am just a temporary foreign worker. They may like send me back or they may stop me any time to work here if I tell this truth to them. (TFW60, male cook from Morocco, working in Newfoundland; NOC 6322, skill level B)

I asked him how this would happen, and he told me, "I decided to not raise the official grievance because I think they may, it may affect my permanent residency process. That's why I didn't do that. I just had to quit." In his case, he would rather be unemployed than do anything that might jeopardize his chance for permanent residency.

The likelihood of a TFW becoming a permanent resident varies according to which stream they belong to. For example, SAWP workers – the largest group of TFWs – are not eligible for any of the programs that are designed to facilitate permanent residency even though SAWP workers frequently have extensive Canadian work experience and may return to Canada repeatedly for the duration of their careers. In contrast, in-home caregivers are eligible for permanent residency after they have completed twenty-four months of working in Canada as part of this TFW stream, as described in the introduction. Between 2009 and 2019, 78,750 caregivers became permanent residents, with the number of transitions peaking in 2016 at 14,200. As a point of comparison, 123,885 work permits were issued through the two in-home caregiver programs that existed during that period (a 64 per cent transition rate).

In contrast, workers in the low-wage and high-wage TFW streams are eligible to use a variety of federal immigration processes, such as the Provincial Nominee programs as well as the Atlantic Immigration Pilot program, to apply for permanent residency status. While the Skilled Trade and Skilled Worker programs are primarily designed for applicants whose work experience was gained outside of Canada, the Provincial Nominee and Atlantic Immigration Pilot programs are designed for applicants whose work experience is Canadian – including but not limited to TFWs. The newer Atlantic Immigration Pilot program first accepted applicants in 2017, and a total of 2,639 applicants transitioned to permanent resident status between 2017 and 2019. The Provincial Nominee programs have existed for longer, and 196,650 people used these programs to transition to permanent resident status between 2009 and 2019, with a peak of 30,040 in 2019. High-wage TFWs are also eligible to apply to the Canadian Experience Class program as a way to potentially transition to permanent resident status, although it should be noted that this program is not available to TFWs exclusively. In total, 145,070 people used the Canadian Experience Class program to become permanent residents between 2009 and 2019.

Immigration, Refugees and Citizenship Canada (IRCC) does not disaggregate TFWs in the high-wage and low-wage programs, but its data suggests that between 2009 and 2019 there were 543,895 TFWs who were either SAWP workers or in-home caregivers. From this, we can infer that not all high-wage and low-wage TFWs are able to transition to permanent resident status through the Atlantic Pilot program, the Provincial Nominee programs, and the Canadian Experience program (see table 4.1). Indeed, setting aside the fact that non-TFWs can apply for these programs, there are a minimum of about 1.5 potential TFW applicants for every available spot, assuming a set rate or quota for successful applications.

The process for TFWs to become permanent residents, if they are eligible, is not necessarily easy or straightforward. Several TFWs who spoke to me were frustrated by the complexity and bureaucracy of the immigration process. Some, for example, were asked to provide information that was difficult to obtain (e.g., the translated and notarized death certificate of an ex-spouse who had moved to another country before passing away). Others had difficulty because of the actions of their Canadian employers. For example, a videographer from Croatia had her application for permanent residency denied because her

Table 4.1 TFW transitions to permanent resident status and TFW permits issued, 2009–19

	Year											Totals
	2009	2010	2011	2012	2013	2014	2015	2016	2017	2018	2019	
Transitions to permanent resident status												
Canadian experience	2,065	2,990	4,720	7,230	5,580	18,660	15,055	12,695	26,760	23,210	26,105	145,070
Atlantic immigration pilot programs	0	0	0	0	0	0	0	0	40	685	1,905	2,630
Provincial Nominee programs	8,985	9,515	9,855	13,200	16,935	17,905	20,185	17,805	20,135	28,090	34,040	196,650
Caregiver	6,330	7,760	5,085	3,750	4,930	11,830	11,400	6,975	9,425	7,170	4,095	78,750
TFW permits issued												
Agricultural workers	31,765	32,240	34,350	35,530	38,075	40,380	40,905	46,560	48,475	53,820	57,645	459,745
Caregivers	23,210	19,345	18,200	13,645	12,145	13,005	7,405	6,710	3,675	3,105	3,530	123,975
Other TFWs (e.g., high-wage and low-wage, higher-skill and lower-skill)	66,115	63,800	70,140	77,555	78,065	46,895	27590	26,940	25,375	25,715	35,705	543,895

employer had not completed his required paperwork properly. He had inappropriately required her to work as an independent contractor instead of as an employee, which meant that she could not submit the T4 slips to the Canadian Revenue Agency to document her work history. This is a violation of the TFW guidelines as well as the Canada Revenue Agency regulations on the differences between employees and independent contractors.[57] As she told me, "Canada as a country, welcoming immigration, and almost like a promised country? That's fake. That's very fake. Canada is not welcoming [to] immigrant[s] and Canada is not easy to immigrate [to]. And it was [a] promised country. So, I don't want to be negative, but I know that Canada is making very good marketing about immigration, but it is not what they say" (TFW30, female videographer and seamstress from Croatia, working in Ontario; NOC 5222, skill level B). Although many TFWs decide to work in Canada because of the prospect of becoming a permanent resident, many are disappointed.

Overall, TFWs make careful comparisons between their different job opportunities in various countries. Rather than simply comparing their career prospects in Canada with their opportunities in their countries of origin, TFWs consider the trade-offs between wages and working conditions in several different countries, and refine their choices as their careers progress and their priorities change. Depending on their stream, many TFWs also choose Canada over other available options because of the prospect of becoming permanent residents.

Employers' Comparisons

My research suggests that some employers also make comparisons between the working and living conditions that TFWs face in Canada and in their countries of origin. They believe that the TFWs they hire tend to have shorter working hours and receive a higher hourly wage in Canada in comparison with their countries of origin or other countries where they are eligible to work. As one Ontario employer told me, "I met many, I think they're thrilled to make it to Canada. One, you're getting a higher wage, a more political, stable country from where these people are originally from. And then most importantly, it's that pathway to get your PR [permanent residency]. I don't know any other country that's going to do that ... better labour law, so shorter working hours, better pay, rights, health coverage. But we need immigrants. With our land and population, we need to fuel the economy. These people want to work" (MAN30, female employer of an in-home caregiver, living in

Ontario). Many employers who spoke to me were pleased that Canada had become an attractive place for TFWs and immigrants; they saw Canadian labour standards as a competitive advantage compared with other countries that might also be recruiting workers.

Unfortunately, these international comparisons may also factor into some employers' decisions about how to treat their TFWs. Some managers reported that their Canadian employees' working or living conditions – which did not meet provincial employment standards – were acceptable because they were better than what the TFWs would have experienced in other countries. For example, I spoke to a farmer in Alberta (discussed in chapter 5) who told me, "Well, where they come from, the number-one advantage to coming here is a steady job that pays well compared to where they're at. And where they are, there basically is no healthcare to speak of" (MAN06, male farmer in Alberta). He felt that his TFWs, who were recruited from Mexico and the Philippines, were automatically better off, just by virtue of being in Canada. Although these workers did not access the Canadian healthcare system while they were in Canada, he felt nonetheless that the presence of Canadian health care was an important consideration. He did not acknowledge that his TFWs had worked in their countries of origin (i.e., that their work experience was the reason why he had hired them), or that there were other countries where they could emigrate for work. He simply felt that any TFW was automatically better off in Canada, regardless of how they were treated. I later asked the owner of a repair company in British Columbia how his TFWs fared in Canada. Like the Albertan farmer, he felt that TFWs benefited from the program and were generally pleased to be in Canada. I asked him why, and he said, "From being able to get a permanent residency, if the job is offered to them long enough. I mean, let's face it. I don't know how, if you were born in this country, but we live in the best country in the world. Absolutely no doubt in my mind about it" (MAN08, male owner of a repair company in British Columbia). In his view, any job in Canada was better than any job elsewhere, because it offered the prospect of permanent residence in Canada. To him, immigrating to Canada was its own reward.

Not surprisingly, some workers reported feeling that their managers were expecting gratitude for having "rescued" them from a low standard of living in their countries of origin. I spoke to one live-in caregiver from South Africa who was working in Alberta. The relationship with her employers had deteriorated because they were preventing her from seeing her friends, they were not paying her the overtime they owed her, and they were requiring her to do a long list of supplementary housekeeping tasks that were not in her job description. I asked her if she felt safe in her current situation and if she had access to her passport as well as a way to leave quickly if she needed to. She told me:

> I don't think they will do something bad to me but I just think that they, you know, they just don't want to lose any money, they want to make the most of having you and they don't realize that, you know, you, I didn't come from a country where I'm dying or my life sucks and they're not saving me from anything and that's kind of what they put me. They kind of make me feel like, that like we did so much for you, we took you out of your Third World country and have [given] you a life in Canada, like you know you should be grateful. And it's just, it's not like that. (TFW10, female in-home caregiver from South Africa, working in Alberta; NOC 4411, skill level C)

This TFW's parents had previously hosted foreign students as part of cultural exchanges, and she was seeking something similar in Canada. She was surprised that her employers were so disdainful and incurious about her country of origin. Although she had originally planned on exploring the option of becoming a permanent resident in Canada, she had since changed her mind and was planning on returning to South Africa or joining her brother in the United States instead. Although her employers felt that she had ended up in Canada because she had few alternatives, this TFW felt otherwise. She believed that she had several opportunities available to her; the Canadian job had not been an enjoyable experience for her, because of the working conditions, so she was going to explore other options that fit better with her expectations.

Conclusion

Canada's reliance on foreign labour is not unique. Many other countries recruit TFWs from the Philippines, India, and Mexico to do in-home caregiving, agricultural labour, and lower-wage and higher-wage work. It behooves us, then, to consider how Canadian working conditions for TFW workers compare with those in other countries. International comparisons are important because workers are mobile and have many countries to choose from. As part of their decision-making process, potential TFWs consider many factors, including wages, working conditions, and the type of work that is available.

A comparison of the regulations and guidelines suggests that the Canadian TFW program is not unlike those available for foreign workers who seek employment in the United States, Australia, and Europe. However, many TFWs perceived that their labour rights in Canada were less robust than the rights available to them in Europe (e.g., the ability to change employers). Conversely, the Canadian TFW program is more regulated than the foreign worker programs in Hong Kong and the United Arab Emirates. However, many TFWs perceive that jobs in Asia pay more than similar jobs in Canada. The TFWs who do choose to come to Canada do so at least in part because they perceive that working conditions in Canada are more equitable.

It should be noted that when TFWs consider the possibility of working in Canada and compare their options in Canada with their options in other countries, the largest differences that they will perceive are likely to be due to the type of work permit they can obtain (e.g., agriculture, caregiving, or any work that does not require an advanced degree vs. work that requires an undergraduate degree or other higher qualifications). For example, there are few differences between the work permits for very highly skilled TFWs in Canada and in the United States, but there are considerable differences between the work permits available to higher-wage TFWs and agricultural workers within Canada.

Although the international comparisons may affect the likelihood of TFWs choosing Canada as a destination, they also have important implications for how TFWs in Canada interpret and make sense of their experiences. Because many TFWs have work experience in their countries of origin or elsewhere before arriving in Canada, their understanding of what constitutes normal treatment has already been formed. However, these underlying assumptions may have unintended consequences. TFWs may not be aware of all their rights in Canada, and may therefore be less likely to contest unsafe working conditions or unfair treatment.

Ultimately, these international comparisons do not matter as much as the employment standards that the Canadian government has legislated. As a society, Canadians have determined that workers deserve certain protections. The specific employment laws vary somewhat by province but they all include provisions for a minimum wage, overtime, maximum hours of work per day/per week, and workplace health and safety. Canadians have also determined that all workers have the same protections, regardless of citizenship or permanent residency. Whether the Canadian TFW program is in fact better or worse than similar programs in other countries doesn't really matter; the situation in other countries is not a reasonable justification for weakening protections for workers in Canada.

Reluctant or Reckless

Canadian Employers' Use of the TFW Program

Considering the widespread and continuing use of the TFW program by a variety of Canadian employers,[1] one might assume that the users of this program are relatively satisfied with its attributes and how it is administered.[2] However, many employers find the program expensive, time-consuming, and difficult to use. Employers usually base their decision to use the program on a variety of factors, including the availability of labour, comparisons of the costs, and the added value of hiring TFWs instead of permanent residents or Canadian citizens. Employers' satisfaction with the program is also affected by several factors, including their short-term or long-term orientation and their attitudes toward the government officials who oversee the program.

In this chapter, I identify and contrast the utility cost considerations for employers that hire employees under the Seasonal Agricultural Worker Program (SAWP), the in-home caregiver program, and the low-wage and high-wage TFW programs. I also present data on the areas in which companies have been cited and penalized for non-compliance with the program. This chapter, then, elaborates on the reasons underlying employers' dissatisfaction with the TFW program, and explains the circumstances in which employers may use these factors to justify their non-compliance. I conclude with a suggested typology of employers: those who are reluctant users of the Canadian TFW program and those who are reckless users of it.

Strategic Human Resource Planning

Every employer needs to make continual strategic decisions about the composition of its workforce, the number of employees it will hire as well as the nature of their employment contracts. For example, if one employee leaves or if the organization's workload has increased to the point that additional labour is needed, the employer must decide whether to pay a current employee overtime, provide additional training to an existing employee, or hire an independent contractor, a temporary employee, or a permanent employee either part-time or full-time. These decisions are not always straightforward.

The primary considerations when evaluating the cost-effectiveness of a particular staffing strategy are the service costs and the service value associated with each individual worker. Although direct costs such as wages, agency fees and other transaction costs, and benefits are more visible than indirect costs such as absences, turnover, training, and health and safety incidents, all must be fully accounted for. Similarly, service value must be calculated on the basis of the workers' task performance as well as their organizational citizenship behaviours (i.e., how much they informally help co-workers or the organization). This procedure is known as a utility analysis. In the research literature, it has been applied to examine the cost-effectiveness of hiring various types of workers.

For example, in a theoretical utility analysis of contingent worker employment practices, Fisher and I examined the cost-effectiveness of three different HR strategies that involved varying proportions, levels of integration, and pay levels of permanent employees, temporary agency workers, and independent contractors (i.e., low cost, core-periphery, and temp-to-perm staffing strategies).[3] Interestingly, this analysis found that the supposedly low-cost strategy of hiring many low-paid temporary workers on the assumption that most will quit or be fired was likely to be less cost-effective than the temp-to-perm HR strategy of paying workers more and transitioning them to permanent employment, because the emphasis on low wages led to higher turn-over costs, which were more expensive in the long run. Turnover costs, incurred when an employer needed to replace a worker (e.g., recruit and select a replacement, incur lost productivity before the new worker arrived or had been adequately trained), were conservatively estimated as being 1.5 times the yearly wage of the employee who was being replaced, in accordance with industry norms.[4]

The considerations for employers that are evaluating the cost-effectiveness of hiring TFWs instead of Canadians or permanent residents are broadly similar to their other strategic hiring decisions about what category of employee to hire, with some variations depending on the stream of TFWs being considered. Below, I describe some of the considerations inherent for each type of worker, taking into account both the unique and shared characteristics of the four different programs.

SAWP Workers

Many of the costs of using the SAWP program are different than they would be to hire employees who are Canadian or permanent residents. Although the wages may be somewhat lower, the employers incur additional costs for housing and for transportation to Canada and to the work site. However, the indirect costs are likely to be far lower. In particular, absenteeism rates are very low, because the SAWP workers typically live on the farm premises. Furthermore, the SAWP workers tend to have lower turnover costs because they frequently return every season for several years. Training costs will also be modest, as SAWP workers are selected because they are highly skilled and experienced. These turnover costs were a key consideration for many of the employers who spoke with me. For example, when I asked a farmer in Alberta why he bothered with such a complicated and expensive program, he explained to me, "That's not the point of it. It's to have somebody there when you go to work in the morning and you don't have to look for them" (MAN06, male farmer in Alberta). He found that the program was an efficient use of his resources simply because it enabled him to hire workers who were much less likely to quit.

The value provided by SAWP workers also differs from that provided by employees who are Canadian or permanent employees. By all accounts, SAWP workers are high performers and agreeable employees who are willing to work overtime. As Leigh Binford notes, many employers suggest that without the SAWP program they cannot compete internationally.[5] The overall net value (i.e., taking into account all costs and value-added) is likely to be higher for SAWP employees than for Canadians or permanent residents.

In-Home Caregivers

The turnover costs of hiring an in-home caregiver who is a TFW or a Canadian or permanent resident are difficult to estimate, because of countervailing factors. On the one hand, TFWs who are participating in the in-home caregiver program will typically stay with their employer for the length of time that is required for them to qualify for permanent residence (barring contract breaches or other mistreatment, as described in chapter 1). However, after this period has ended, they are likely to quit and seek other employment (e.g., in a long-term care home). Thus, most in-home caregivers who are TFWs can be expected to leave after about twenty-four months, which may or may not match the employer's needs. In comparison, in-home caregivers who are Canadian or permanent residents may turn over more frequently, but the timing of their turnover would be unrelated to their citizenship transition process.

Further to these costs, employers who hire TFWs must pay a $1,000 application fee to be considered for a Labour Market Impact Assessment (LMIA), in addition to the necessary wages and any agency fees. The employer must also provide accommodations that comply with the TFW guidelines (e.g., sufficient square footage, window, lockable door). If a suitable room does not already exist, then renovations must be completed at the employer's expense. Comparing the costs of hiring a TFW and an applicant who is a Canadian or a permanent resident is complicated, however, by the fact that most applicants who are Canadian or permanent residents insist on living elsewhere (i.e., in their own homes), and an employer cannot insist that an in-home caregiver live in the employer's residence, only that they perform their work there. Thus, while the accommodation expenses (e.g., living space, food, Wi-Fi, utilities) of an in-home caregiver who is a TFW would be identical to the accommodation costs of a Canadian or permanent resident as long as the worker was living in the employer's residence, it is unlikely that a Canadian or permanent resident would agree to this arrangement. In-home caregivers who do reside with their employers (i.e., TFWs) are also less likely to be absent or late for work, which reduces the costs of temporarily replacing them (e.g., lost wages from a parent missing work to care for a child, wage costs for hiring a short-term replacement).

The tendency of in-home caregivers who are TFWs (but not Canadians or permanent residents) to reside with their employers is likely to lead to higher performance assessments for these employees, because their employers are likely to perceive them as being more available to work longer hours and more flexible about when they work those hours. Thus, the net value provided by TFWs who participate in the in-home caregiver program is likely to be higher than that provided by Canadian or permanent resident employees.

Low-Wage TFWs

For low-wage TFWs, many of the direct costs, such as wages, should be similar to what they would be for employees who are Canadian or permanent residents because employers must pay TFWs the median wage for the industry and region where they are located. However, some of the direct costs may differ. When hiring a low-wage TFW, employers must pay a non-refundable fee of $1,000 to apply for an LMIA, a fee they do not incur when hiring a Canadian or permanent resident. Furthermore, employers who are seeking TFWs may also incur the costs of hiring an agency or an immigration consultant to assist with recruitment and paperwork.

These elevated direct costs may lead many employers to consider the TFW program expensive and time consuming. For example, the owner of a property management company that specialized in the hospitality and tourism industry told me, "I'd be surprised if anybody who worked with the foreign worker program thought that the foreign worker was cheaper in the end than the Canadian one, because it just wasn't the case. By the time you paid for everything, the foreign worker was more expensive, but we were so desperate we needed to have them" (MAN13, male owner of a property management company in British Columbia).

However, according to many employers, the indirect costs of training tend to be lower for TFWs than they are for employees who are Canadian or permanent residents. Even for relatively skilled positions, training needs will be minimal because most TFWs will have significant work experience before being selected for work in Canada. For example, a TFW who works as a cook in a Canadian quick-service restaurant may have extensive experience working on cruise ships, where food safety regulations are stricter and more consistently enforced, and where a greater variety of cooking techniques are required. TFW training, therefore, will only focus on local requirements (e.g., recipes for house specialties) rather than foundational skills. In contrast, the non-TFW applicants for low-wage jobs tend to be less experienced and require more significant training. In an economic analysis comparing the behaviours of TFWs and Canadian employees, Brochu, Gross, and Worswick found that TFWs work longer hours, have lower rates of absenteeism, and are less likely to be laid off.[6] They attribute these differences to the fact that TFWs have fewer alternative employment options.

The indirect costs of absences and turnover will also be lower for TFWs than they will be for Canadians or permanent residents. Despite the short-term nature of the TFW program, TFW employees are likely to stay until the end of their contracts because it is difficult for them to switch employers. In contrast, Canadian and permanent residents are likely to have higher turnover rates because they can easily seek alternative employment elsewhere. Many employers report that TFWs also have lower absenteeism rates. This further contributes to their lower employment costs compared with other employees. For example, when I asked one slaughterhouse owner in Saskatchewan why she didn't hire more Canadians, she responded, "There were a few rejects, and I say that with all respect, from Alberta that couldn't find work there and had a hard time living in Calgary and Edmonton. They'd find their home in rural Saskatchewan and maybe buy a $10,000 home here, but they were all drug related. And so we hired a few of those, and I'll tell you what. That was just a disaster" (MANI5, female owner of a slaughterhouse in Saskatchewan). Her comments echo the findings of a study by Gravel and her colleagues who suggest that employers believe that TFWs are perceived to be more loyal, more competent, and more likely to stay for the entire season than local Canadian workers.[7] They note that Canadian workers are more unreliable and are more likely to be late or absent, possibly due to drug or alcohol problems.

Interestingly, Gravel and her colleagues found that employers seek TFWs to ensure that they have a reliable and steady workforce. These findings were drawn from a 2017 study of Quebec employers' experiences with the low-skilled TFW stream. These employers were from several industries, including agriculture, horticulture, and laundry.[8] Furthermore, as noted by Polanco,[9] employers in the fast-food industry are especially likely to perceive TFWs as more energetic and customer-oriented than employees who are Canadian or permanent residents. Indeed, according to many employers, low-wage TFWs have high levels of performance, which the employers attribute to higher levels of experience and motivation, even though TFWs may not be familiar with local social norms or cultural expectations. Employers also note that low-wage TFWs who are seeking permanent residency in Canada are frequently hoping to have this process facilitated by participating in the provincial nominee programs, as described in chapter 4. Thus, they endeavour to be perceived positively by their employers. Taken together, these factors may contribute to a somewhat higher net value for TFWs.

High-Wage TFWs

The costs for high-wage TFWs will be broadly similar to those for Canadians or permanent residents, with the exception of the $1,000 LMIA fee and other agency or immigration consultant costs required only for hiring TFWs. It should be noted that the LMIA fee is a small proportion of the overall direct costs, because the other associated costs are so much higher; this fee is a less important consideration for employers of high-wage TFWs than it is for employers of low-wage TFWs. Moreover, turnover costs are a more important consideration because they are calculated as a function of the employee's annual salary or wages (i.e., 1.5 times the salary costs of the employee who leaves). Turnover tends to be lower in higher-wage industries, so high-wage TFWs are less likely to turn over than low-wage TFWs. However, compared with Canadian or permanent resident employees, high-wage TFWs are less likely than to leave during their initial contracts – although they may be more likely to leave if they become permanent residents. It is therefore difficult to estimate the indirect costs of hiring high-wage TFWs and to compare these costs with those incurred when hiring other types of employees.

The performance levels of high-wage TFWs compared with their Canadian or permanent resident counterparts are also difficult to estimate, because both groups of employees are likely to be highly trained and experienced. The value of these workers' contributions will largely depend on management procedures (e.g., recruitment and selection, compensation) and leadership behaviours, so it is highly variable. However, research in Australia by Wright and Constantin[10] suggests that highly skilled TFWs are perceived by employers as being more productive than domestic employees, thus making them more cost-effective.

Overall, the cost-effectiveness of hiring a TFW instead of a Canadian or permanent resident will depend on several factors. According to Gravel and her colleagues,[11] employers do not hire TFWs to lower their wage costs. Rather, they hire TFWs to reduce their overall labour costs because TFWs are high performers and are willing to be flexible about when they will work. According to Gravel's research, this flexibility is multifaceted; it refers to the employer's ability to have (a) the exact number of workers and the exact number of labour-hours available when needed; (b) workers available for the exact schedule needed, that is, available to work during the day, evening, night, weekend, or split shifts; (c) workers willing to be paid in the cheapest possible way, including hourly, by piece work, by volume, or by task; and (d) workers who are able to perform multiple tasks.[12] Although Gravel's research was conducted in Quebec, it is interesting to consider that Knott found similar employer preferences among New Brunswick seafood process-ing plants,[13] and my own interviews for this book uncovered similar views among the managers from across Canada who spoke to me.

The Financial Impact of Employers' Non-Compliance

The above discussion about the financial implications of hiring TFWs instead of Canadian or permanent resident job applicants assumes that the employers will be complying with the TFW program regulations. That is, employers will pay their TFWs the agreed-upon wages – including all overtime and holiday pay – and avoid requesting any illegal fees or other payments from them. It also assumes that employers will pay the indirect costs of some of the TFW streams, such as providing suitable accommodation for workers in the SAWP and in-home caregiver programs. As discussed in chapter 1, it is clear that not all employers comply with these legal requirements.

However, it is difficult to estimate the proportion of employers that are non-compliant for various reasons or engaging in wage theft specifically. Qualitative data and reports from advocacy groups are useful in identifying that the practice exists and is relatively common, but this type of evidence is not designed to aid in determining the precise proportion of employers that engage in this behaviour. For some idea of the prevalence of the different types of non-compliance, a census or statistically representative survey of TFWs' experiences would be required. In the absence of this type of data, it is useful to examine the list of employers who have been found non-compliant. Between 2017 and 2020, 273 employers were found to be non-compliant for a variety of reasons, including a lack of appropriate documentation; this information is summarized in table 5.1.

Of the employers who have been investigated and cited for non-compliance, the percentage engaging in wage theft is less than one third (27 per cent or 75/273). Indeed, most of the citations result from employers not complying with the documentation required to participate in the program. There can be significant financial consequences for non-compliance; fines are levied for more serious breaches of the guidelines. Between 2016 and 2020, a total of $707,000 in fines was levied against employers, with the average fine being $3,258.06 during this period. There are employers who engage in wage theft who have not yet been investigated for non-compliance, but based on the available data, we can infer that for the majority of employers wage theft is not part of their official HR strategy.

Table 5.1   Non-compliant employers, 2017–20*

	2017	2018	2019	2020	Totals
Total number of violations recorded	48	48	114	63	273
Total number of fines	21	24	109	63	217
Total value of fines	$81,500	$81,250	$361,000	$183,250	$707,000
Maximum fine imposed	$54,000	$21,000	$30,000	$49,750	
Number of temporary bans imposed	27	25	8	0	60
The employer couldn't show that the information they listed in the offer of employment was true, for a period of 6 years, starting on the first day the temporary worker worked for them.	2	3	10	5	20
The employer didn't keep documents that showed they met the conditions of employing a temporary worker, for a period of 6 years, starting on the first day the temporary worker worked for them.	1	0	4	1	6
The employer didn't have the money to pay the wages agreed to with a live-in caregiver.	0	0	0	0	0
The employer couldn't show that the description they gave for the job on the LMIA application was true, for a period of 6 years, starting on the first day the temporary worker worked for them.	0	1	2	1	4
The employer didn't show up for a meeting with the inspector, to answer questions and give documents the inspector asked for.	0	1	2	3	6
The employer didn't give the inspector the documents they asked for.	3	7	74	45	129
The employer didn't show up for an inspection and didn't help or give information to the inspector when asked to.	0	1	2	3	6
The employer broke federal, provincial, or territorial laws for hiring and recruiting employees in the province or territory where the temporary worker worked.	0	1	2	2	5
The pay or working conditions didn't match, or were not better than, what was listed on the offer of employment, or the job was not the same as what was listed on the offer of employment.	18	13	35	9	75

	2017	2018	2019	2020	Totals
The live-in caregiver wasn't living in a private home in Canada or was not providing unsupervised care for a child, or senior or disabled person within the home.	0	0	0	0	0
The hiring of the temporary worker didn't create new jobs or job stability for Canadian citizens or permanent residents.	0	0	0	0	0
The hiring of the temporary worker didn't result in Canadian citizens or permanent residents obtaining new or improved skills and knowledge.	0	0	0	0	0
The employer didn't hire or train Canadian citizens or permanent residents as agreed.	0	0	0	0	0
The employer didn't put in enough effort to hire or train Canadian citizens or permanent residents, as they agreed.	0	0	0	0	0
The employer was not actively engaged in the business that the temporary worker was hired to work for (aside from live-in caregivers).	0	4	11	2	17
The live-in caregiver didn't receive private and furnished living space in the home.	0	0	0	0	0
The employer didn't put in enough effort to make sure the workplace was free of any of the following: physical, sexual, psychological, and financial abuse.	0	0	1	1	2
The employer stopped the foreign national from complying with an order or regulation made under the Emergencies Act or the Quarantine Act.	0	0	0	0	0
The employer stopped the foreign national from complying with a provincial law that governs public health.	0	0	0	0	0
The employer didn't provide wages to the foreign national that were substantially the same as those set out in the offer of employment, during the period the foreign national was required to isolate or quarantine on entry into Canada.	0	0	0	3	3
The employer didn't provide the foreign national with accommodations that were separate from those provided to persons not in quarantine, and that permitted the foreign worker to remain at least 2 meters away from any other person.	0	0	0	0	0

	2017	2018	2019	2020	Totals
The employer didn't provide the foreign national with cleaning products for the purposes of cleaning and disinfecting the accommodations regularly.	0	0	0	0	0
The employer didn't provide a foreign national, who developed any signs or symptoms of COVID-19, with accommodations that had a bedroom and a bathroom solely for the use of the foreign national while they isolated themselves.	0	0	0	0	0
The employer didn't provide adequate accommodations to a foreign national employed to perform work under an international agreement on seasonal agricultural workers between Canada and one or more countries.	0	0	0	0	0
No reason is recorded because the employer was found non-compliant for an incident that occurred before new regulations came into effect in 2015.	27	23	6	0	56

* Government of Canada, "Employers Found Non-Compliant."

Reacting to the Local Labour Market

Rather than being concerned about reducing labour costs, many of the employers who use the TFW program were more concerned about the availability of labour. Part of the issue appears to be a perception that local applicants are unmotivated and will not perform well. For example, a report by Fang and colleagues on the availability of labour in Labrador notes that employers characterize local employees as "lazy."[14] Likewise, a separate report by Knott echoes these themes, noting that local workers are no longer preferred, and that TFWs are considered to be the "right" kind of employees.[15] However, several of the managers who spoke with me also cited the fact that they needed to hire workers with specialized expertise, and that these workers were difficult to recruit in Canada. For example, the owner of a map publishing company said he would post job advertisements but the Canadian applicants were entirely unqualified. As he explained:

We've had people apply to us to work, saying, "Oh yes, I did cartography. I took an hour-long course of it in university." I said,

"That's nice and my wife took five years learning cartography and
you did it all in one term, isn't that wonderful, you're brilliant!
You're also incompetent!" Because there is no way you can learn
cartography in one term ... people say, "Well, oh don't you do any
training?" I say, "How can I train you? It takes five years to learn
how to be a cartographer at university. How can I train you in six
weeks?" (MAN04, male owner of a map publishing company in
British Columbia)

This publishing manager felt that he needed a TFW with specialized
expertise to keep his business afloat, and, in his experience, this expertise
was not available in Canada.

Indeed, most managers who spoke with me noted a variety of external circumstances that reduced their ability to hire Canadians, which
was a necessary but not sufficient condition for their use of the TFW
program. A recurrent theme among managers was that geographic
considerations affected the supply of available workers. This concern
was particularly salient for companies in the tourism and hospitality
industry. They required a fairly large number of employees, but the
companies were not located in highly populated regions, and there
were frequent infrastructure problems (e.g., poor road conditions in the
winter, no mass transit) that prevented people from commuting from
other areas. As a manager of a hotel in British Columbia explained:

You had to post the jobs for Canadians and prove that you
couldn't get Canadians to apply, or [that] you couldn't get the
right kind of applicants. We had positions sitting empty for
literally years. We could not find anybody who wanted to come
at all. We were constantly just posting the position. And it's
because resort areas are very different than a usual town where
people, you know, they live, their families grow up. Resort towns,
a lot of people come here temporarily ... And so it's not like a
normal working environment in a big city, for sure, because
we just don't have the labour pool, and it's not like other small
towns where you have families that live there, that have multiple
generations there. You know, when you have 40 per cent of your
housing maybe lived in four weekends of the year and summer
holidays or something, it's like those people aren't going to work
in your community. (MAN13, male hotel and property manager in
British Columbia)

This manager preferred to hire Canadians, but he had considerable difficulty doing so. He was paying above-market wages, but the local supply of labour was limited, so he was using the TFW program to meet his staffing needs. Other managers in even more remote communities faced similar challenges. For example, I spoke to one manager of an adventure tourism company in Manitoba who would have preferred to hire Canadians because he felt that tourists expected to meet Canadians when they travelled to Canada. However, this was difficult for him to accomplish. One of the primary attractions of his hotel and tour operation was its location in an isolated region of Canada that had abundant wildlife. Unsurprisingly, the population of his town was less than 1,000 people. The working-age population was much lower, and the people who lived there were already employed. For his company to grow, he needed to hire more staff, but finding the relevant expertise locally was unlikely, and the nearest town was about 400 kilometres away. This manager was reluctant to hire TFWs, and he had scaled back his use of the program as much as possible, but it was crucial for his staffing strategy.

However, some managers cited external circumstances that seemed less insurmountable. One owner of a fast-food restaurant in New Brunswick explained to me that he needed to use the TFW program to find employees because he was not able to recruit employees locally. I asked him why this was the case, because his restaurant was in a mid-sized city with fairly high unemployment.[16] He told me that a river ran through the centre of town, and it was impossible to recruit staff who lived on the other side of the river:

> [City] is delineated by the [River], which separates the West Side from the rest of the city. And this is my assessment: nobody crosses the bridge for what I call an entry-level job. You're not crossing the bridge to work at [a restaurant] or fold jeans at [a store] or pour coffee at [a restaurant] or drop fries at [a restaurant] or any of those entry-level jobs. You're crossing the bridge to work at the [factory], you're crossing the bridge to work at the [factory] and the [factory], the mid- and upper-level jobs. But the entry-level positions, people aren't taking that journey ... And that part of the city, like I say, it's a micro market within the market, and people just don't cross over for those jobs. And it's not just [restaurants]; they don't cross over to work at [restaurants] or [stores] or stock shelves at [stores] or any of the

grocery stores. If you're working in an entry-level position you're not going to commute long distances to do that job. (MANO7, male restaurant owner in New Brunswick)

I was skeptical about the extent to which the geography of his city was actually affecting his ability to recruit Canadian employees. I believe that the wages and working conditions that he was offering (and that were under his control) were more relevant. It is worth noting that this particular manager was taken to the Labour Board by some of his employees because he was not providing them with their mandated breaks. However, he felt that his actions were justified and reasonable because of his perception of how the river affected employment in his city.

Overall, it is difficult to argue that managers' beliefs that external circumstances have pushed them to use the TFW program are causing them to abuse the program.[17] Every company manager that uses the TFW program must explain to the federal government that they are justified in doing so because they cannot hire Canadians to do the work. However, a close examination of the words used by the managers to describe their use of the program is instructive. In particular, it is interesting to compare how managers discuss the problem of finding suitable employees. The hotel manager in British Columbia (MAN13) displays personal responsibility in his framing of the recruitment challenge. For example, he states "*We* could not find anyone" (emphasis added). In contrast, the restaurant owner in New Brunswick (MANO7) puts the emphasis on what others do; he states that "*people* just don't cross over for those jobs" (emphasis added). Some managers took responsibility for managing the staffing process, whereas others blamed external factors for any difficulties that they were having.

There was a tendency among non-compliant managers to claim vociferously that labour market circumstances dictated their inevitable use of the TFW program, while omitting to mention their own failures in recruiting employees or in developing succession plans. It is possible that this sense of external factors being the most important consideration in hiring TFWs may have contributed to a perception among some managers that it was permissible to cut corners regarding their use of the program.

Employer Evaluations of the TFW Program

Most managers who had used the TFW program were widely dissatisfied with it. For example, there was a fairly universal consensus among the managers that the program was unreasonably slow. As one Alberta farmer told me, "They're less than slow!" (MAN06, male farmer in Alberta). The TFW program, in fact, has become slower over the years as it has become more complicated. The government officials who administer the program need to assess the genuineness of the employer's need to hire TFWs, the appropriateness of the compensation and other benefits (e.g., accommodations for the workers), as well as the employer's plan to transition away from using this program to meet staffing needs (depending on the stream). There is typically some clarification that is required during this process, which delays the application further.

The owner of a sports academy in Ontario described the process this way:

> You have to do your advertising. You have to submit the application into the government, which can take from what I recall, it can take a couple of months before you hear any feedback, and then you go back and forth with them. Then once you get notification, you need to let the foreign worker know, and then they have to get their visa from their home country, which can take another month, and then wrap up whatever they're doing there because they might be working there. So then they have to give notice and make arrangements to come, which could take another month or so. So by the time they actually could get here, it could be like six months. (MAN10, female owner of a sports academy in Ontario)

I asked her how long she thought the process should take, and she said, "That timing is way too long. I would say timing needs to be around two months' turnaround." Most of the managers found that the entire TFW process took about six months (although there seemed to be a range of about three to nine months, albeit much longer in some cases) but they thought a two-month-long or three-month-long process would be more reasonable. Many managers unfavourably compared the length of time needed to go through the TFW approvals with the time required for other government approvals, such as receiving a passport (which requires security checks) or receiving business licences.

However, it is interesting to consider how managers responded to the slowness of the program. While some managers were resigned to dealing with the inconvenience of the timelines, others may have been using it as an excuse for not following the letter or the spirit of the guidelines. A wide variation in how managers reacted was evident in my interviews with them. Taken together, a picture emerges of a bureaucratic program that is slow to approve the applications of TFWs who want to work in Canada. Unfortunately, it is possible that some managers, perhaps those with more short-term orientations, use the slowness of the program as a way of rationalizing trying to cut corners. For example, they may not advertise the job for as long as or as widely as is required, or they may fail to accurately document the number and characteristics of the Canadian applicants and why they could not be hired.

I spoke to a hobby shop owner who would plan about one year ahead to take into account the delays that he anticipated from the TFW program administrators (MAN02, male hobby shop owner, Ontario). Although this was perhaps an extreme example, several other managers reported having implemented rolling recruitment several times each year to cope with their staffing demands. As the manager of a garden nursery told me, "We're at the point where we know we always need helpers. We've set it up so that we bring in several different timeframes for a year, so that if we actually do end up with some Canadians that are willing to work then we don't necessarily have to bring all the guys we request in but, we have to start, yeah, five, six, seven months ahead of time. So it's not practical, but at the same time I don't see a way around it. So we've made it work, I guess" (MAN09, male garden nursery owner in Ontario).

The owner of a sandwich restaurant told me how he always planned ahead: "For the summer, I've already got a plan in place. So what my next plan is going to be [for] October, November when I know a couple of people are going to be leaving, you know? So I have to come up with a plan where I am able to replace them. You always plan for six months, for the next six months" (MAN12, male sandwich restaurant owner in British Columbia). These managers planned ahead for every aspect of their businesses (e.g., supplies, inventory, taxes) and thus extended this planning to cover their staffing needs.

The employers' adjustments to their staffing strategies were initially time consuming to develop. The owner of a hamburger restaurant also in British Columbia told me that "you're used to hiring in the short run, not in one-year segments. And so I just find the length of time it takes to get somebody on the ground and actually working, it's just too long" (MAN11, male hamburger restaurant owner in British Columbia).

He therefore developed completely different approaches to how he
hired the Canadians that he needed for one of his restaurants, and
how he hired TFWs for another of his restaurants in a more remote
tourism area where he found it more difficult to recruit locally. He hired
Canadians and permanent residents on an as-needed basis, and expected
them to begin work as soon as possible, but he started planning about a
year in advance to recruit his TFWs from the Philippines, a process done
in batches on an annual basis. As with other managers, the restaurant
owner explained to me that he would prefer the TFW hiring process to
take about three months or so, but because this was not possible, he
had adapted his hiring practices accordingly.

However, some managers adapted by bending the spirit if not the
letter of the TFW guidelines. Similar to the above-mentioned hamburger
restaurant owner (MAN11), they advertised on the Canada Job Bank
well in advance of when they needed someone, to meet the minimum
requirements of the TFW program. However, they did not ever expect
any Canadians or permanent residents to apply for these jobs because
they were (intentionally) advertised so far in advance of when the jobs
would start. They would *not* then advertise again locally once their TFWs
were in place. I asked a tree nursery owner in Alberta why he didn't
advertise, even though the TFW guidelines stipulate that he needs to.
He told me:

No, we don't advertise because really, even advertising, the way
we have to advertise for Service Canada, honestly, it doesn't make
sense because you're hiring labourers, and so those people are at
minimum wage in Alberta, $13.60. If we hire someone in January
and we tell them work starts April 5, the likelihood is that person
is not going to be waiting. It's a different thing to hire someone
to become a VP and he's going to make $150,000. But the labourer
really needs the job now, and so if we cannot give them the job,
anyone else that's going to pay him $13.60, or her $13.60, they're
going. So we just really start to advertise in December so that we
can meet the regulations of Service Canada. But when we have
to put on the application, when I send my application to Service
Canada, I have to tell them how many people, how many replies
we got from our advertising, and then how many people we hired
out of that advertising, and how many we refused and for what
reason. And mostly the thing is very few people apply because
they need money now. They need to work now. They're not going
to wait three months. And $13.60 working outside, I don't think
tempts them too much. And like they want to work now. So we

just try to advertise a few weeks before the start of the season. And then usually we don't advertise [again] because if we lose one or two workers, two others can pick up the slack. (MAN14, male tree nursery owner in Alberta)

I asked him if it was truly the case that he didn't advertise all his open positions, because the TFW guidelines clearly require companies to advertise the open positions to Canadians. He responded, "Yes. You have to advertise, so that's why we start in December, because on [the] Job Bank of Canada and anywhere you have to advertise for a minimum of one month for your application [to] be looked after." In this case, he found the TFW program to be too slow to approve his hiring, so he felt justified in creating a parallel system where he (1) advertised most jobs unreasonably early so that he would not be likely to be able to hire any Canadians; (2) used the inevitable lack of applications as a justification to hire many TFWs; (3) advertised a few jobs locally closer to when he might expect the Canadian workers to be available to start work; and (4) avoided advertising positions when they became available later in the season, opting instead to not fill those positions. This process violates the spirit of the TFW guidelines, but this manager felt justified in doing so because he felt that the TFW program was too slow to meet his needs.[18]

Overall, it is difficult to know exactly how much the managers' short-term orientation contributes to their abuse of the program. Many industries are fast-paced and routinely deal with high employee turnover and chronic staffing shortages. Non-compliant managers tended to assert that the timelines in the TFW program were completely unreasonable, while minimizing their own failures to plan ahead. In contrast, the most compliant managers accepted the timelines as inconvenient but part of their normal planning processes. It is possible that a short-term orientation may have contributed to a perception among some managers that it was acceptable to skip some of the steps in the process that they would have to follow to use the TFW program.

Employer Attitudes toward Government Regulations

Another frequent concern managers raised was that the government did not understand their business well enough to regulate it. In some instances, government National Occupation Classification (NOC) codes did not exist that could adequately describe the job that was vacant. For example, there was no way to explain that the company needed to hire a "Master Cheesemaker," that is, someone with several years of post-secondary training and work experience in making cheese. This was an important consideration, because the alternative NOC codes would incorrectly imply that the employee would have either managerial duties (i.e., if a NOC code was selected to put the wages at a reasonable level) or do menial labour (i.e., if a NOC code was chosen to represent the fact that the work would happen on a farm).

A related complaint among farmers was that the government did not understand modern farming, and it therefore tried to treat each field or orchard on the farm as though it were a separate business (e.g., the government treated different locations on their farms as equivalent to different franchises in a restaurant chain). The farmers pointed out that the Canada Revenue Agency treated all their fields (or orchards) as part of a single business for taxation purposes, but that the administrators of the TFW program did not necessarily come to the same conclusion. The government's shifting or variable interpretation of the parameters of the business's locations had important implications because the TFW guidelines stipulate that TFWs cannot be moved between different businesses. If the farm's various fields were separated geographically, then moving the workers between them would either be entirely acceptable (according to the farmers who believed that a modern farm could have several fields) or against the TFW guidelines (if the fields were considered to be separate farms). It was difficult for the farm owners to seek clarification on this matter.

Most managers expressed at least a casual disdain for "the government" while they were telling me about their experiences with various aspects of the TFW program. For example, the owner of a repair company in British Columbia told me, "Oh yeah, it's a typical government program. The people that design it and run it don't have a goddamn clue what they're doing" (MAN08, male repair company owner in British Columbia). A parent who employed an in-home caregiver[19] told me, "I have to tell you, government doesn't seem at all interested in the employer's perspective. Like zero interest" (MAN28, female employer of an in-home caregiver in Ontario). In her case, she felt that the government did not appreciate the demands on families who hired caregivers, and she resented the fact that the government was not providing viable childcare alternatives for dual income families. This resentment was a frequent theme in my interviews. As the Alberta farmer explained, "I don't think they have any background in business. They don't seem to know how a business functions" (MAN06, male farmer in Alberta). This farmer was irritated that the government was going to audit his use of the program. He told me, "They're coming and doing an audit! I mean, what purpose does it serve, other than to make sure that they're looked after?[20] They're looked after here 100 per cent." I was, in fact, skeptical of the extent to which his employees had fair and safe working conditions, because he had seemed disappointed that he was not permitted to house his workers in his granary. However, this employer felt that the government officials had insufficient expertise or experience to evaluate his employment practices or his use of the TFW program.

Some of the managers had negative views of the public servants who administer the TFW program; they were considered to be naive and biased. The owner of the map publishing company believed that "government people are people who've never worked, so they have no idea what it's like to be in the workforce … they have very little understanding of how the world works outside of Ottawa" (MAN04, male owner of a map publishing company in British Columbia). He felt that the government workers were so out of touch with contemporary Canadian business practices and needs that they were not qualified to determine who could use the TFW program or how they could use it.

The most positive statements I heard were from managers who had tempered their expectations of the government workers that they dealt with while using the TFW program. As the owner of a landscaping company in British Columbia explained to me, "In the past, if [you] wanted to talk to Immigration you [would] talk to somebody in Immigration. And you could be talking to somebody who was a fairly expensive person. The government several years ago when they set up Service Canada said, 'We're going to have a bunch of people who can fill in the forms.' And that's all they are. So you can't expect very much from them" (MAN25, male landscaping company owner in British Columbia). He was impressed that the government had reorganized the department so that lower-paid employees could answer most of the public queries, because he felt that this was a more efficient use of human resources. However, he also felt that the quality of customer service he received was much lower, and that it was difficult to receive nuanced answers to his questions about the program.

Some managers also derided the government for its failure to audit companies that were failing to use the TFW program properly. As the hamburger restaurant owner in British Columbia explained:

> You get some abuses there where they could have hired locally, but they did not and they hired a foreign worker and pleaded that they couldn't find anybody. And that does happen. And so that's a hot button. And then you've got a large labour union saying,

'Oh, you're not giving Canadians a chance,' and all that kind of stuff. And some of those things are true ... no matter what you do, you're going to get people who try to avoid taxes illegally. And so I wish the government would do audits and understand the various locations that have problems. (MAN11, male hamburger restaurant owner in British Columbia)

This sentiment suggests that government efforts to monitor the use of the TFW program have the immediate benefit of directly increasing employer compliance, but they may also have a further benefit: increasing the credibility of the government with employers who use the program, which may also increase employer compliance.

The TFW Program Helps TFWs (Too Much?)

Workers are naturally in the best position to determine whether or not they benefit from the TFW program, but many managers noted the many ways in which the workers they hired benefited from this experience. Through their employment, TFWs often gained specialized work experience that they could use to advance their careers in Canada or elsewhere. Many were able to improve their non-technical skills, such as their English-language abilities and understanding of Canadian workplace culture; Canadian experience was frequently seen as being crucial in securing future employment in Canada. Many employers believed that the wages and working conditions were better in Canada than elsewhere. The managers were very aware, too, that the TFWs were often working in Canada to provide better opportunities for their children. As the owner of the garden nursery explained to me:

For most of these guys, it's a way for them to help advance their families, and that's probably one of the biggest things we hear from them. Some of the fellows that we have working here, at home they're making $5 to $7 a day. So something like this allows them to build a house, it allows them to send their kids to school. Several of our guys have been here for nine, ten, eleven years now. They're sending their children to university now, so they're getting degrees, they're getting educated. Most of the ones that work here probably had school only to the age of eight to ten, on average, years old. So very, very poor education. This really gives their families a leg up. (MAN09, male garden nursery owner in Ontario)

However, some managers seemed to believe that the TFWs benefited too much from their participation in the program. Indeed, among some managers there was a sense that the TFWs should be more grateful for the opportunity to work in Canada. The owner of the family farm in Alberta, who had been hiring TFWs for many years, described to me the work that they did on his farm. He was very satisfied with their work, and he considered them to be higher performers than his Canadian employees, but he believed that the TFWs were becoming more entitled now. I asked him how his experience with the program had changed over the years, and he responded:

> I was thinking about some people that came to work for my dad
> years ago, and my dad had a big old granary in the back, and
> they were a German family. They came like in the fifties. And my
> dad put a couple of beds in the granary and put a stove in there
> and some cupboards in there, and they stayed in the granary
> all summer till they got a house to live in. And their name was
> [name]. And [name], he worked for us twenty-five years, and his
> brother worked for us four or five years, and his dad went to that
> [city] area and they got a farm there and they had two different
> farms, and those kids all did really well. But they had a place
> to start, eh? My dad give them a few jobs there and give them a
> place so they can get their feet under them, and away they went.
> But they wouldn't live in a granary today. (MAN06, male farmer
> in Alberta)

This farmer seemed to put his TFWs into a different category than his Canadian workers. He expected them to be more humble, more grateful, and less demanding, and he seemed to take credit for their eventual successes. At no point did he suggest that his Canadian employees should live in the granary.[21]

The owner of the repair shop was upset that the TFWs he hired were not more grateful for the opportunities that he had provided for them. At first he spoke more generally, telling me:

> I think that they adapt fairly well, but part of the problem that I
> see is that the idiot that you have in Ottawa right now or we have
> in Ottawa right now, it's indentured upon him that they have
> all these rights. My attitude is you don't have any rights in this
> country until you contribute for at least a generation. You don't

come into somebody's house and then tell them to start moving the furniture around and start changing this and make sure you're delivering a couple of drinks as soon as they get in the house. You basically have some humility and some gratefulness that you're here, and you contribute. (MAN08, male repair company owner in British Columbia)

I asked him more specifically how this applied to the workers he had hired over the years. He told me that one of his recent TFW hires had now become a permanent resident, which seemed to have changed how they related to each other. Whereas they previously had a good working relationship, their interpersonal dynamic had shifted once the employee was no longer a TFW. The employer explained, "I mean, like his daughters are both, one's in post-secondary education, the other one is I think heading into high school. His wife's a top seller at the car dealership she's at. It's one of the problems is you can't even talk to him now. He's the big shot. You know, he's incredibly arrogant, but you know, he won't give anybody else credit for that. He figures he's done everything and you can't talk to him." On the one hand, this employer did not want former TFWs to fail to "contribute" before asserting their human rights, but on the other hand he also did not see the TFWs as his equals and he did not want their success to exceed his own.

It is difficult to assert that managers who believe that TFWs benefit disproportionately from the opportunity to work in Canada are necessarily non-compliant with the TFW guidelines. For example, the employers described above did not identify any ways in which they mistreated their employees or violated the regulations for the use of the TFW program. However, their comments are troubling, and suggest that at least some Canadian employers do not see TFWs as deserving of the same rights as other people.

Conclusion

The answer to why employers use the TFW program is not always straightforward. The evidence from my interviews with managers who are using the TFW program confirms that they do not focus exclusively on wage costs, and instead take into account several factors. The TFW program is expensive and time consuming to use, and recent changes mean that employers must pay TFWs at least the average median wages usually paid to Canadians in that occupation in that region. However, many managers believe that using the TFW program can still provide the employer with overall cost savings because they believe that TFWs are more productive and have lower turnover than Canadian workers.

Unfortunately, some employers may be using the ongoing problems with how the TFW program is administered as excuses for not following all its guidelines carefully. As explained in chapter 1, many of the TFW regulations are broken. Indeed, I spoke to several employers who had been "blacklisted" or found to be non-compliant with the TFW guidelines after being audited by the government. Companies that are non-compliant may pay a monetary penalty, and they may also be banned from hiring TFWs in the future.[22] Approximately 375 companies have been found to be non-compliant for a variety of reasons, and the details regarding their non-compliance are listed in table 5.1. At the time of writing, the largest fine levied was $220,000. Some employers have been permanently banned from hiring TFWs.

The question of why managers sometimes *abuse* the TFW program is complicated.[23] Most – but not all – of the managers who spoke with me were, in fact, completely compliant with the TFW program. Based on the evidence from my interviews, it appears that compliance is time consuming yet still achievable. However, managers who had a highly short-term orientation, were disdainful of the government's authority to run the TFW program as it saw fit, felt that circumstances beyond their control were to blame for their staffing problems, and minimized the hardships faced by TFWs in Canada, were more likely to be non-compliant with the TFW guidelines. Managers who planned ahead, accepted the government's authority to run the TFW program (even if they were still critical of the government, public servants, or politicians), took responsibility for their organization's staffing challenges, and acknowledged the hardships faced by TFWs in Canada were less likely to be non-compliant. Problematic managers tended to have a pattern of cognitions that they could use to rationalize non-compliance. Each factor was insufficient, by itself, to guarantee that a manager would be non-compliant, but a picture emerges of two general types of managers: *reluctant users* of the program, who were resigned to following all its rules no matter how inconvenient, and *reckless users*, who saw their use of a TFW program as their right as business owners who needed to solve some immediate staffing problems.

The reluctant users of the program fully recognized the need for close oversight of how and how many TFWs they brought to work in Canada. Many would ideally prefer to hire Canadians, and most had made ongoing efforts to do so, but they had also realistically assessed the feasibility of relying exclusively on Canadians, so they often tried to support the efforts of their employees who were TFWs to become permanent residents. They considered the expense and time that they spent on managing their use of the TFW program to be normal costs of doing business in their region or industry. There was also a sense that non-compliant competitors were receiving an unfair advantage; the reluctant users felt that better enforcement of the guidelines would result in a level playing field where the rules would apply equally to everyone.

In contrast, the reckless users of the program tended to feel that the public scrutiny of the TFW program was overblown, and that the program had been unnecessarily curtailed in recent years. They believed that it was impossible to hire qualified Canadians, and they felt that TFWs were much easier to manage. These managers asserted that the bureaucracy of the TFW program was so complicated that no one could comply with it. The fact that most employers are indeed able to comply with the TFW guidelines suggests that compliance is possible, but that enforcing and monitoring this carefully is crucial.

6

Conclusions

An Enduring Program for Enduring Work?

The Canadian TFW program is controversial. Given its unpopularity with employers, TFWs, and the general public, it is not surprising that a number of suggestions have been put forward to either amend it or abolish it. In this chapter, I address several of the recommendations that have been suggested by employer and TFW advocacy groups, as well as the employers and TFWs who spoke to me. Given the diversity of stakeholders, no solution will please everyone. However, given the sustained problems with the current TFW program, it is worth considering the advantages and drawbacks – from employers' as well as TFWs' perspectives – of open or occupation-specific work permits, additional opportunities for TFWs to apply for permanent residency, immediate permanent residency, and several other administrative changes.

Open Work Permits

One promising modification to the TFW program would be to abolish closed work permits in favour of either open work permits – so the successful applicant can work for a set period of time for any employer anywhere in Canada – or occupation-specific work permits – which are similar except that the successful applicant can only work in the occupation for which they received approval. Cedillo, Lippel, and Nakache[1] suggest that occupation-specific work permits for TFWs offer advantages over the aforementioned pathway to citizenship alternative. Specifically, they note that TFWs who depend on their employers' roles in the immigration process are less able to voice concerns about how they are treated. The authors thus assert that occupation-specific work permits reduce the likelihood of disparities between the TFWs' written contracts and their actual conditions of work.

Interestingly, the distinction between open work permits and occupation-specific work permits may be spurious. When applying for a new job, TFWs are far more likely to be limited by their work experience and qualifications as well as their own geographical constraints than by any federal restrictions on the occupations to which they may apply. Moreover, as explained in chapter 1, the available occupational codes (i.e., NOCs) do not always map neatly onto the actual jobs that are posted; for example, the duties of a cook (NOC Code 6322, skill level B) may overlap significantly with those of a chef (NOC Code 6321, skill level B), kitchen helper (NOC Code 6711, skill level D), or food service manager (NOC Code 0631, skill level O). Employers may use the codes selectively (e.g., choose a code that is for an occupation that is more in demand) to improve their odds of a successful Labour Market Impact Assessment (LMIA) application.

However, adding layers to a bureaucratic process of ensuring that work permit NOC codes match precisely is an unnecessary burden for employers and TFWs alike. From an economic standpoint, the increased labour mobility of TFWs moving into more valued occupations (i.e., those that are paid more) is desirable because it allows labour resources to flow to the employers who require them most, and it places economic pressure on employers to improve their pay and working conditions to attract more job applicants. From a practical perspective, open work permits give employers the flexibility to promote TFWs as their skills develop.

Open work permits are currently provided to TFWs who alert the government that they are being mistreated; this flexibility provides them with the opportunity to pursue alternative employment while remaining in Canada, and to continue to pursue permanent employment if they so choose. As it stands, the number of TFWs who use this provision is low. By expanding this initiative and providing flexibility to all TFWs, these workers will be able to proactively remove themselves from dangerous situations or from employers that are not honouring their employment contracts.

This middle ground, offering a compromise between providing permanent residence upon arrival and the current closed work permits, has been criticized by business advocacy groups such as the Canadian Chamber of Commerce.[2] These advocates note that the costs of using the TFW program are not insignificant, and they suggest that employers will avoid hiring TFWs with open work permits. Their underlying concern is that employers believe that the costs of hiring TFWs will no longer be offset by lower turnover rates – because the TFWs will use their open work permits to seek employment elsewhere. However, employers who are confident in the pay, working conditions, and living conditions (if applicable) that they provide would be likely to continue using the program, although they may need to adjust their recruitment and selection strategies. For example, it would behoove them to provide more detailed and realistic job previews, have more stringent selection criteria, and recruit a larger number of TFWs with the assumption that some will leave. Furthermore, some employers may benefit from being able to recruit skilled TFWs from competitors where there is a poor match between the TFWs and the employer or where the TFW is being mistreated.

Taking this initiative further, it may be useful to consider situations where a TFW could maintain employment at their initial employer, while also pursuing employment either at a second location of their current employer or at a different employer altogether. This option is currently unavailable. Likewise, additional flexibility could be provided for the TFW to be promoted or to assume additional responsibilities (for higher compensation) that were not stipulated in the original contract. As it stands, this flexibility is not provided, to prevent an employer from advertising an intentionally unattractive job (e.g., limited job duties, low compensation) to demonstrate that no Canadians will apply for it – so they can be permitted to hire a TFW and then improve the job to a standard that would appeal to Canadians interested in applying.

Because of the time and effort that is taken up applying for permission to hire TFWs, employers would benefit from having the choice to extend contract lengths so they can provide workers with more time to complete their applications for permanent residency. In this regard, it would be somewhat similar to the European Blue Card program (discussed in chapter 4). Most TFWs would be pleased to extend their contracts with their original employers because of the costs and effort required to either switch jobs or return to their countries of origin. Allowing employers to extend contracts could be an incentive for them to treat TFWs well so that they do not leave, thereby allowing employers to recoup their investment in their recruitment costs. For this process to be viable, the federal government would need to track the number of TFWs who stayed at their original employers despite having an open work permit. Employers who had a high proportion of TFWs leaving, whose TFWs always left after becoming permanent residents, or whose TFWs lodged complaints against them, would receive more scrutiny (e.g., more audits, requests for more information, added attention to future LMIA applications).

A Clearer Path to Permanent Residency

Another option, which could be implemented simultaneously, would be to provide all interested TFWs with permanent residency after a set period of time working in Canada (e.g., after two years, as with the in-home caregiver[3] program), or to expand the availability of current programs for existing TFWs in specific industries or regions who seek permanent residency. The idea of a clearer path to permanent residence has been suggested as an alternative to the current TFW program by business advocacy groups, such as the Canadian Federation for Independent Business, Restaurants Canada, and the Hotel Association of Canada.[4]

Increasing the opportunities for TFWs to apply for permanent residence would build on current initiatives, such as those for the year-round agri-food industry (e.g., mushroom farms, meat processing)[5] or the Atlantic Immigration Pilot program.[6] Historically, workers who participate in the Seasonal Agricultural Worker Program (SAWP) stream have not been eligible to apply for permanent residence but enabling them to be eligible may help to address chronic labour shortages and an aging workforce in certain industries. A larger number of TFWs could also be made eligible to apply for permanent residency by subsuming some or all streams of the TFW program into the International Mobility Program, which is geared toward workers with university education who reside in countries that have a comprehensive trade agreement with Canada.

This option preserves the process for recruiting and vetting employers and workers who seek to use the TFW program (e.g., the LMIA process does not change). The onus for navigating the permanent residency process is on the individual worker, although some employers may provide support to facilitate this process. It does not necessarily decrease the bureaucracy of the current TFW program and all its attendant costs. However, employers benefit significantly from increased access to qualified employees because the prospect of permanent residency is attractive to many job applicants even if it would not be granted immediately upon arrival.

Unfortunately, it is not clear that this arrangement would necessarily protect TFWs; they would still be vulnerable during the period between their arrival and when they would be granted permanent residence. As described in chapter 1, the in-home caregivers who spoke to me and who were entitled to permanent residence at the end of their contracts endured a lot; the *prospect* of permanent residence did not protect them. Moreover, one TFW who spoke to me, a truck driver, was fired when his employer found out that he was about to become a permanent resident. In this case, he could readily seek employment elsewhere, but his experience counters the general narrative of employers *always* trying to use the TFW program as a way of recruiting permanent employees who will become permanent residents.

Moreover, looking at the numbers in table 4.1, it is clear that not every TFW who applies for permanent residence is accepted. While these programs are popular with employers and prospective immigrants alike, their availability is problematic if these pathways offer only the possibility of permanent residence rather than providing it in practice.

Immediate Permanent Residence

Some worker advocacy groups, such as the Migrant Rights Network, have suggested that all TFWs should be offered permanent residence upon arrival in Canada.[7] Although the details proposed by different groups vary, the core element of this recommendation is that the category of TFW be eliminated in favour of simply providing permanent residence immediately to those who work or live in Canada.

For employers, the primary advantages of this approach arise from its utility in making Canada a more desirable destination for potential job applicants. Canada is already an attractive prospect for many potential immigrants, as described in chapter 4, but the ability to provide job applicants with the opportunity to receive permanent residence automatically would represent a competitive advantage for Canadian employers who compete with employers in the United States, Australia, or Europe for comparatively qualified employees. Employers who would have used the low-wage TFW program would also be especially likely to benefit from the opportunity to hire the increased numbers of new permanent residents who initially came to Canada to work for a particular organization but who are, in fact, eligible to work anywhere and for any employer. This "poaching" is likely to put some upward pressure on wages.

Unfortunately, employers would likely still need to use a fairly bureaucratic process that would be similar to the one they deal with currently. The current LMIA process allows employers to assert that they will facilitate the permanent residency of the TFWs they hope to recruit rather than developing a transition or succession plan whereby the TFWs transfer their knowledge and skills to Canadians. This aspect of the LMIA process could be amended, but employers would likely still need to demonstrate they need to recruit from abroad, which can be complicated and time consuming. Because of the irrevocability of the end result (i.e., permanent residency rather than a temporary work permit), the fees, the documentation requested, and the time required for the application process will likely continue to be significant, if not become more so.

For workers, however, the prospect of immediate permanent residence is very attractive. Without the constraints imposed by the closed work permit, these individuals can easily quit their jobs and move anywhere in Canada to seek employment elsewhere. The increased mobility also offers societal economic advantages; by moving jobs more frequently, a better match can be made between employee qualifications and the needs of employers. These workers would also have immediate access to community and social supports that are currently restricted to immigrants. Most important, they would be less vulnerable to threats or mistreatment from employers.

However, as with open or occupation-specific work permits, increases in workers' mobility is also the primary disadvantage for employers if the TFW program were to be overhauled in favour of providing workers with immediate permanent residence. As described in chapter 5, a key reason why it is sometimes cost-effective to hire TFWs (despite the costs of accessing this program) is the low turnover rates of TFWs compared with other types of employees. If workers' turnover rates increase because their permanent residence gives them more employment opportunities, then employers may be more reluctant to hire these workers, given the other costs involved.

Perhaps the most serious disadvantage of offering immediate permanent residence to those who seek to work in Canada is that this would represent a fairly large shift in Canadian immigration policy. Rather than focus on a human-capital approach that prioritizes applicants with educational profiles that match Canadian needs, eligibility for immigration would be determined primarily by employers. This is problematic because employers naturally have significantly different interests and goals than the Canadian government. As a result, employers would naturally advance their own interests by recruiting employees who meet their own needs. In some cases, the recruited workers would fit a similar profile to those who are currently admitted by the Canadian government. However, in other instances, the employer will recruit workers who are not broadly employable but who are willing to accept low wages or poor working conditions in exchange for permanent residence.

Furthermore, employers would not be required to maintain employment for the workers (i.e., new permanent residents) that they recruit. Unless a comprehensive administrative process was created, there would be few barriers to prevent employers from continually recruiting workers from abroad, only for these workers to quit or be fired, and to be replaced by another wave of new recruits. The likelihood of illegal employment fees also increases, because employers would be able to offer workers actual permanent residence (rather than simply the prospect of this) in exchange for a fee. An extensive administrative apparatus could potentially be put in place to mitigate these concerns, but this would necessarily increase the administrative burden for employers and applicants, thereby reducing the savings inherent in a more streamlined process.

Although Canadian employers have an important role to play in civil society, it is not clear that they should influence Canadian immigration patterns so dramatically.

Administrative Changes

To offset the increased employer costs of open TFW permits, several changes should be made where possible to make the application for the LMIA more efficient for employers. First, the process for approving (or turning down) applications for LMIAs should be accelerated. As discussed in chapter 5, the LMIA process is too slow to meet employers' needs. Although the lengthy LMIA approvals process may be deliberate, as a disincentive for employers to use the TFW program, or unintentional, because the federal government is scrutinizing applications more thoroughly now, the net consequence of the slow turnaround times is that some employers would hire fewer Canadians because they would hire more TFWs (in batches) as a bulwark against eventual staffing shortages caused by program delays.

To facilitate quicker processing, it would be helpful for employers to have the option to pay a supplementary fee to expedite processing. For example, for double the usual cost (i.e., $2,000 instead of $1,000), employers would receive a decision on their application within two months. Employers would need to have a clean record of using the program in the past to be eligible for expedited processing, similar to the NEXUS pass or expedited passport renewals. There is a danger that increasing the fees will harm TFWs because these fees seem to be frequently passed on to the TFW, as seen in chapter 1, but this unintended consequence could be mitigated by more careful monitoring of the program, more frequent contact with TFWs, and the increased flexibility afforded by the open work permits. Unsurprisingly, some business lobby groups have advocated for LMIA fees to be refunded in cases where applications are rejected, but this is inadvisable because the fees serve to recoup the administrative costs of the TFW program (which are not diminished when an application is unsuccessful) and act as a disincentive for submitting incomplete or unpersuasive applications.

Second, along with quicker LMIA processing, employers would benefit from more transparency in the status of their applications. Employers and TFWs should be able to log into a secure website to see an automated update of where their file is in the process (e.g., is information outstanding, is it being reviewed, is a decision pending) as well as an estimate of how much longer they will likely have to wait for a decision. This will enable them to plan for the arrival of the TFW (e.g., putting housing in place, planning orientation programs) well in advance.

Third, the LMIA application process should be modified slightly to take into account available NOC codes that are inaccurate descriptors of the focal jobs. The NOC codes are in the process of being revised and the new system will have six categories of codes rather than four. It is currently being used by Statistics Canada and it will soon be implemented by Employment and Social Development Canada (ESDC).[8] How well the NOC codes represent different occupations is crucial because they are used to identify whether the TFW will be in the low-wage or high-wage program, as well as what their wage will be. An "other" option on the list of NOC codes that can be used should be added, which would trigger an alternative consultation process and adjudication of the LMIA. In this case, the employer would indicate up to three NOC codes that most closely matched the job description, and justify which one (or the average of which ones) should be used to calculate the local median wage. This alternative process would require more explanation and oversight, but it allows employers to be more accurate and descriptive about the job duties.

Additional Protections for TFWs

The introduction of open work permits will not eliminate TFWs' mistreatment. Additional protections should be introduced that focus on both preventing and halting non-compliant behaviours, as well as monitoring TFWs' experiences carefully so that further changes to the administration of the program can be implemented.

Protection from Family Members

One of the groups of TFWs who are most vulnerable are those who are employed by their own extended family members, as seen in chapter 3. Right now, the federal government does not appear to track this information. However, the LMIA application forms could be amended to enable ESDC to monitor these TFWs' working and living conditions more carefully. More specifically, the current application forms for LMIA currently request that employers complete a Temporary Foreign Worker Information Template that provides information on the workers who are likely to be hired (e.g., name, date of birth, country of residence). This form could be modified to require employers to indicate how the employee is known to them (e.g., through a recruitment agency, a friend or family member of a current employee, a friend or family member of someone in a leadership role in the organization). Indicating that the potential employee is a friend or family member of someone in a leadership role in the organization would not be grounds for denying the application, but it could invite further scrutiny, either of the application or of the experiences of the worker once they arrive in Canada. As with other documents that are submitted as part of the TFW program, lying on this part of the TFW application form would be grounds for a warning, a fine, or becoming ineligible to hire future workers.

Reduce the Cost of Mistreatment Complaints

Much of the mistreatment faced by TFWs is somewhat mundane and will never make headlines. For example, if TFWs do not receive their promised overtime pay or holiday pay they are unlikely to seek redress beyond asking their supervisor or HR department (if they have one) to pay them. However, these violations of employment standards are still inherently problematic, and they represent a slippery slope that may lead to other violations (e.g., health and safety breaches). The cost of reporting (e.g., in time, money, and hassle) has to be low enough for it to be worthwhile for the TFW to take action, even when the cost of the mistreatment is small (especially in relation to the potentially enormous cost of the employer finding out and retaliating). The federal government therefore needs to make its complaint-driven process simpler to use, as well as implement more robust and frequent independent audits. Interestingly, employers generally support stronger penalties for employers that are non-compliant.[9]

The TFWs who spoke to me were often reluctant to lodge complaints about their mistreatment because they feared retaliation. They were concerned that the government would label them "troublemakers" and bar them from receiving permanent residency. They were also concerned that their employer would find out about their complaint and then fire them, which would also potentially affect their permanent residency applications. The government website needs to be clearer about the protections that can be offered to TFWs who complain about their employers. It would be useful to encourage former TFWs to lodge complaints about any incidents that occurred within the past two years of their employment. Many of the TFWs I spoke with had kept extensive documentation of their mistreatment, including copies of their pay stubs and bank statements as well as correspondence with their employers.

Furthermore, as discussed in chapter 5, the federal government does audit employers' compliance with the TFW regulations. However, additional transparency about how companies are selected for audits would give the public more confidence in this process. Introducing spot checks and surprise audits would be useful because they provide plausible deniability for current employees who complain in confidence. In fact, many employers (the "reluctant users") who spoke to me welcomed the opportunity to demonstrate to the government that they were following all the relevant regulations; they believed that others (the "reckless users") should do the same and generally felt that a small number of non-compliant businesses were damaging the reputations of employers in their industries or regions. Although some audits could be done remotely (e.g., requests for documentation), audits that are conducted in person provide a more comprehensive sense of the TFWs' physical surroundings (e.g., smell of mould, noise levels, room temperatures, security, crowding, safety equipment and procedures). As an added layer of protection, the federal government should endeavour to use an automated "push" notification to connect with each TFW. This could be done by contacting the TFW at least once during the year they are employed in Canada, and once more after their contract has ended (e.g., after the TFWs have returned to their country of origin or become a permanent resident and remained in Canada). The push notifications could be sent, by ESDC, via text, phone, or email, to help ensure that only the TFW – not their employer – would see the communication. The automated survey could ask the TFW to respond to a very brief questionnaire (e.g., questions about whether their contract is being followed). If the survey reveals that the TFW regulations are not being followed, then the federal government would know to scrutinize the employer more closely.

Safer Housing

Unfortunately, as seen in chapter 1, the housing or accommodation provided to TFWs as part of their contracts is sometimes grossly inadequate. This situation is complicated by the fact that multiple levels of governments are involved. There are municipal standards for building requirements, but provincial employment standards and public health offices as well as federal rules also determine where TFWs can and cannot live. Because effective coordination between the different levels of government may not be possible, the federal government should assume that no other government body is intervening, and then audit and enforce its own rules accordingly.

At issue is the fact that the in-home caregivers, low-wage, and SAWP programs each have a separate set of regulations about the housing that is provided to TFWs, but each set of regulations is different.[10] For example, the SAWP program requires employers to provide suitable housing and have an inspection report completed by the appropriate provincial, territorial, or municipal body or by an authorized and certified private inspector. SAWP employers must ensure that the number of workers in each housing structure does not exceed the maximum occupancy permitted. They must also ensure that sufficient housing will be made available for all the TFWs they employ from their date of arrival to their date of departure. In contrast, employers of low-wage TFWs are only responsible for providing or ensuring that suitable and affordable housing is available. On the LMIA form, the employer must simply indicate the cost of the rent, the type of housing (e.g., rooms in a house, an apartment, a dorm), the number of bedrooms, the number of occupants (including the TFW), and the number of bathrooms.

The regulations for the in-home caregivers are the most specific, and they can therefore be applied to the other TFW streams. On the LMIA form for in-home caregivers, employers must indicate the length and width of the bedroom where the TFW will stay, and the form notes that the total area must exceed nine square metres. The bedroom must also include a door that can be locked (with a safety bolt) from the inside as well as from the outside, with the key provided to the TFW; a secure exterior window that closes and locks from within; finished ceilings, floors, and walls; a bed with mattress and bedding (e.g., sheets, pillows, blankets); lighting; heating; and a closet. Any other amenities that are offered (e.g., telephone, television, cable or satellite, Internet) must also be listed, and they become part of the contract. These regulations can easily be extended to other types of TFWs. There is no reason why a hotel cleaner or an agricultural worker should require less living space than a nanny. Likewise, all TFWs would benefit from having a window, as well as a secure place to store their belongings.

Unfortunately, during the recent pandemic, concern grew about the safety of TFWs, especially those who worked on farms in British Columbia and Ontario. British Columbia introduced new quarantine procedures to reduce the risks for TFWs, and there were no reported deaths among TFW farm workers.[11] Many of these procedures were later implemented in Ontario.[12] However, the fact that several TFWs died[13] from COVID-19 in Ontario in 2020 suggests that the safety concerns were valid; these workers lived in farm bunkhouses where physical distancing was difficult and they faced pressure from employers to work even when they were sick.[14] Some TFWs were discouraged from leaving farm property, which made seeking health care difficult or impossible.[15] Between April and October 2020, Ontario farms experienced repeated COVID-19 outbreaks on; 1,364 TFWs (or 5 per cent of the farm worker population) tested positive, approximately ten times the proportion of positive tests in Ontario during the same period.[16] There have been repeated calls to shut down the Canadian TFW program, as recently as the beginning of the COVID-19 pandemic in the early months of 2020. For example, New Brunswick temporarily banned TFWs from entering Canada,[17] and Alberta suspended large sections of the TFW program as part of its economic recovery plan.[18] These provincial governments were reacting to popular concerns that TFWs would take away jobs from Canadians during a period of high unemployment. Nonetheless, each provincial government eventually decided that the program would continue to operate, to maintain Canadian food security and economic interests.[19]

Licensing Agencies and Immigration Consultants

Although the increasing complexity in the LMIA application process is designed to improve oversight of the TFW program, the complexity itself encourages both TFWs and employers who find the LMIA process to be too time consuming and too risky to complete independently to use agents and immigration consultants. It is unlikely that the LMIA process can be streamlined, but clearer information about program requirements and how to complete the government forms may reduce TFWs' and employers' reliance on agencies and consultants.

A TFW will turn to an agent or consultant, for example, when they are unsure of whether they were eligible for the different streams of the TFW program, what jobs they may be qualified for, or how to represent their qualifications accurately. In the course of my research, I spoke to many TFWs who had received advice and support from agencies and immigration consultants that did not meet their needs or was misleading (see chapter 2). For example, they were encouraged to lie about their military service or job qualifications. Furthermore, some TFWs paid fees to agencies in exchange for help in finding a job, even though this practice is prohibited. As a result, many had to turn to community support organizations that were available in their communities for some basic information about program requirements. It would therefore be useful to provide funding to community support organizations specifically for assisting TFWs, in addition to the permanent residents who are their primary clients. Many of the community organization directors who spoke to me acknowledged that, because of the existing funding structures, they have been required to restrict their assistance to permanent residents instead of TFWs (e.g., language classes, assistance understanding their rights).[20] Because many TFWs need help, it would be more useful perhaps to consider them as future permanent residents rather than as transient workers who are not deserving of assistance.

Employers also expressed disappointment in their experiences with agencies and immigration consultants. As noted above, employers often seek advice and direction from agencies and consultants to help process their applications or even recruit TFWs for them. Unfortunately, many employers are disappointed by the value provided by these services; they frequently find that the fees they are charged are excessive and still result in unsuitable workers. More stringent regulations for agencies and immigration consultants that were harmonized across provinces would reduce confusion for users of the TFW program. In 2018, British Columbia introduced the *Temporary Foreign Worker Protection Act*, which requires recruiters and employers to be registered. Manitoba and Saskatchewan have similar requirements. It makes sense for these regulations to be adopted nationally.[21]

Conclusion

If a program that allows employers to recruit workers from abroad is economically necessary, then it is equally necessary to ensure that these people are safe and treated fairly. Unfortunately, so much evidence suggests this is not always the case. The mistreatment that TFWs can face is sometimes compounded by their interactions with unethical agencies and immigration consultants. In some cases, family members can offer social support and informational resources, but when the TFW works for a family member their likelihood of being mistreated is even greater. The Canadian TFW program is not that different from similar labour mobility programs in other developed countries, except that some streams of the Canadian TFW program offer the prospect of permanent residency. This prospect is sufficiently attractive that many TFWs endure considerable hardship to obtain it. The fact that some employers misuse the TFW program means that additional resources need to be devoted to monitoring employer adherence to the government regulations.

The way Canadians allow TFWs to be treated is inherently important, but this also has implications for Canadian workers. Once an employer has an established pattern of mistreating TFWs (e.g., not paying overtime or holiday pay, unsafe working conditions, requiring kickbacks) without any consequences, it is likely that they will continue this behaviour with other vulnerable workers (e.g., workers with disabilities, early-career workers, racialized and Indigenous workers). The Canadian Temporary Foreign Worker Program is likely to continue, and it is up to us to ensure that the workers and employers who use this program can benefit from what it has to offer rather than simply having to endure it.

Notes

Introduction

1 For more information, see the Organizational Behavior Division of the Academy of Management at http://obweb.org/about-us/about-the-ob-division.
2 For more information, see the Human Resources Division of the Academy of Management at https://hrdiv.org/about-us/new-item5.
3 Government of Canada, "2018 Annual Report."
4 Leo, "Waitresses in Saskatchewan Lose Jobs."
5 Campbell, M. "Migrant Mushroom-Farm Workers File Lawsuit and Call for Stronger Labour Protections in Ontario," *Globe and Mail*, 10 April 2019, https://www.theglobeandmail.com/canada/article-migrant-mushroom-farm-workers-file-lawsuit-and-call-for-stronger/.
6 Tomlinson, K., "How an Immigration Scheme Steers Newcomers into Canadian Trucking Jobs – and Puts Lives at Risk," *Globe and Mail*, 11 October 2019, https://www.theglobeandmail.com/canada/article-foreign-truck-drivers-canada-immigration-investigation/.
7 Fudge and MacPhail, "Temporary Foreign Worker Program."
8 André, "Seasonal Agricultural Workers Program."
9 Ibid.
10 Barber, "Domestic Service (Caregiving)."
11 Bakan and Stasiulis, "Foreign Domestic Worker Policy."
12 Bakan and Stasiulis, *Not One of the Family*.
13 Fudge and MacPhail, "Temporary Foreign Worker Program."
14 Pfeffer, "Rise in Foreign Temp Workers."
15 Gross, "Efficient Temporary Foreign Worker Program."
16 Ibid.
17 Ibid.
18 Canadian Council for Refugees, "Evaluating Migrant Workers Rights."

19 Mexico was added to the TWF program in 1974 and is now the largest source of employees.

20 Government of Canada, "Hire a Temporary Worker through the Seasonal Agricultural Worker Program: Overview."

21 Government of Canada, "Hire a Temporary Worker through the Seasonal Agricultural Worker Program: Program Requirements."

22 Employment and Social Development Canada, "Labour Market Impact Assessment Application Seasonal Agricultural Worker Program."

23 Canadian Centre for Occupational Health and Safety, "OH&S Legislation."

24 Employment and Social Development Canada, "Labour Market Impact Assessment Application Seasonal Agricultural Worker Program."

25 Government of Canada, "Hire a Temporary Worker through the Seasonal Agricultural Worker Program: Overview"; Lenard and Straehle, *Legislated Inequality.*

26 Lenard and Straehle, *Legislated Inequality.*

27 Government of Canada, "Live-in Caregiver Program."

28 Government of Canada, "Hire a Temporary Worker as an In-home Caregiver: Program Requirements."

29 Employment and Social Development Canada, "Labour Market Impact Assessment Application In-Home Caregiver Positions."

30 Government of Canada, "Hire a Temporary Worker as an In-home Caregiver: Wages."

31 Employment and Social Development Canada, "Labour Market Impact Assessment Application In-Home Caregiver Positions."

32 Government of Canada, "Hire a Temporary Worker as an In-home Caregiver: Program Requirements."

33 Ibid.

34 In 2016, 19,727 Labour Market Impact Assessments (LMIAS) were approved for higher-skill TFWs.

35 Employment and Social Development Canada, "Labour Market Impact Assessment Application High-Wage Positions."

36 Ibid.

37 Ibid.

38 Ibid.

39 Ibid.

40 Ibid.

41 Government of Canada, "Refusal to Process."

42 Employment and Social Development Canada, "Labour Market Impact Assessment Application Low-Wage Positions."

43 Ibid.

44 Restaurants Canada, "TFW Program Changes Cap Calculation."

45 Government of Canada, "Refusal to Process."

46 Employment and Social Development Canada, "Labour Market Impact Assessment Application Low-Wage Positions."
47 Ibid.

Chapter One

1 Vosko, "Legal but Deportable."
2 Binford, *Going to the Harvest.*
3 Akhtar et al., "Health Wanted."
4 McLaughlin, Hennebry, and Haines, "Paper versus Practice."
5 Vosko, "Legal but Deportable."
6 Oxman-Martinez, Hanley, and Cheung, "Live-in Caregivers Program."
7 Fudge and Tham, "Dishing Up Migrant Workers."
8 Valiani, *Rethinking Unequal Exchange*, 90.
9 Polanco, "Globalizing 'Immobile' Worksites."
10 Strauss and McGrath, "Temporary Migration," 204.
11 Cedillo, Lippel, and Nakache, "Health and Safety of Temporary Foreign Workers."
12 Fudge and Tham, "Dishing Up Migrant Workers," 3–4.
13 Strauss and McGrath, "Temporary Migration," 200.
14 Ibid., 202.
15 For clarity, I am cross-referencing terms in the text to indicate the name of the new stream introduced in 2019 followed in brackets by the old name of the stream in use before 2019: in-home caregiver (live-in caregiver).
16 Robillard et al., "'Caught in the Same Webs.'"
17 For clarity, I am cross-referencing terms in the text to indicate the name of the new stream introduced in 2019 followed in brackets by the old name of the stream in use before 2019: high-wage (higher-skill).
18 Interestingly, this dichotomy ignores the fact that approximately 30 per cent of low-skill TFWs became permanent residents within five years after their arrival, as calculated in 2014, according to Prokopenko and Hou, "How Temporary?"
19 Lenard and Straehle, *Legislated Inequality*, "Introduction."
20 When I spoke to this worker he was part of the higher-skill TFW stream. However, the wages associated with his position (i.e., $36.92/hour, on average, in Quebec) would have led it to be considered part of the high-wage stream (i.e., greater than $22.00/hour in Quebec).
21 This visa was replaced with the Temporary Skill Shortage (TSS) visa in March 2018.
22 Boucher, "Measuring Migrant Worker Rights Violations."
23 Cedillo, Lippel, and Nakache, "Health and Safety of Temporary Foreign Workers."

152

24 Government of Canada, "Hire a Temporary Foreign Worker."
25 The wages associated with this position would have led it to be considered part of the high-wage TFW stream had she applied to use it in 2019 or later (i.e., the median wage for a medical sonographer in Canada was $36.00/hour, well above the median Saskatchewan wage of $24.52/hour).
26 The minimum wage in Saskatchewan increased to $11.32/hour from $11.06/hour on 1 October 2019.
27 Government of Canada, "Occupational Health and Safety."
28 The wages associated with this position (i.e., $40.00/hour on average in Alberta) would have led it to be considered part of the high-wage TFW in 2019, because they exceed the median wage in Alberta ($26.67/hour) at that time.
29 Preibisch and Otero, "Does Citizenship Status Matter?"
30 Ibid.
31 The rate of pay for chefs in Manitoba ranges from $12.00/hour (low) to $23.50/hour (high) with the median wage being $15.00/hour. There is thus a chance that this higher-skill TFW's wages would be lower than the Manitoba median wage (i.e., $21.00/hour), meaning that if he were hired after 2019, he would be considered a low-wage TFW.
32 The median wage for videographers in Ontario is $27.18/hour. This higher-skill TFW would therefore have been hired into the high-wage TFW stream if she had been hired in 2019 or later, because the median wage in Ontario is $23.08/hour.
33 Boucher, "Measuring Migrant Worker Rights Violations," 290.
34 Binford and Preibisch, "Interrogating Racialized Global Labor Supply."
35 Skrivankova, *Between Decent Work and Forced Labour*, 25.
36 Mackey et al., "Dark Side of Leadership."
37 Waldman et al., "Predictors of Abusive Supervision."
38 Zhang and Bednall, "Antecedents of Abusive Supervision."
39 Barnes et al., "'You Wouldn't Like Me.'"
40 Byrne et al., "Depleted Leader."
41 Fudge and Tham, "Dishing Up Migrant Workers."

Chapter Two

1 Fudge, "Global Care Chains."
2 Employment and Social Development Canada (ESDC), "Labour Market Impact Assessment Application High-Wage Positions"; ESDC, "Labour Market Impact Assessment Application In-Home Caregiver Positions"; ESDC, "Labour Market Impact Assessment Application Low-Wage Positions"; ESDC, "Labour Market Impact Assessment Application Seasonal Agricultural

Worker Program"; Government of Canada, "Code of Professional Conduct";
Strauss and McGrath, "Temporary Migration."

3   This cost is $1,000 for most employers. Some exemptions are available
    (e.g., users of the SAWP agricultural program and employers of in-home
    caregivers who have incomes below $150,000). This is an application fee, and
    it is not refunded if the request for permission to hire a TFW is denied.

4   Airfare will vary depending on the time of year and the locations.
    Based on 2019 rates: round-trip airfare between Manila and Toronto is
    approximately $850; it is $800 between Manila and Vancouver. Round-trip
    airfare between Mexico City and Toronto is approximately $665; it is about
    $775 between Mexico City and Vancouver. Round-trip airfare between Delhi
    and Toronto is approximately $1,305; it is about $1,195 between Delhi and
    Vancouver. Airfare within Canada (e.g., connecting flights from a major hub
    to the end destination) will also vary in price.

5   Jensen and Meckling, "Theory of the Firm."

6   Eisenhardt, "Agency Theory."

7   Villegas, *North of El Norte*.

8   Strauss and McGrath, "Temporary Migration"; Preibisch and Hennebry, "Buy
    Local, Hire Global."

9   C. Bains, "B.C. Supreme Court Certifies Foreign-Workers Lawsuit," *Globe and
    Mail*, 19 September 2017, https://www.theglobeandmail.com/news/british-
    columbia/bc-supreme-court-certifies-foreign-workers-lawsuit/article36319696/.

10 K. Tomlinson, "False Promises: Foreign Workers are Falling Prey to a
    Sprawling Web of Labour Trafficking in Canada," *Globe and Mail*, 5 April
    2019, https://www.theglobeandmail.com/canada/article-false-promises-how-
    foreign-workers-fall-prey-to-bait-and-switch/.

11 A. Dharssi, "Workers Without Borders: Part 3 of 6 Exploiting the Workers,"
    Vancouver Sun, 20 September 2016, NP2. Note that I am using the term "in-
    home caregiver" to also refer to live-in caregivers.

12 M. Campbell, "Migrant Mushroom-Farm Workers File Lawsuit and Call
    for Stronger Labour Protections in Ontario," *Globe and Mail*, 10 April 2019,
    https://www.theglobeandmail.com/canada/article-migrant-mushroom-farm-
    workers-file-lawsuit-and-call-for-stronger/.

13 K. Tomlinson, "How an Immigration Scheme Steers Newcomers into
    Canadian Trucking Jobs – and Puts Lives at Risk," *Globe and Mail*, 5 October
    2019, https://www.theglobeandmail.com/canada/article-foreign-truck-drivers-
    canada-immigration-investigation/.

14 Cundal and Seaman, "Canada's Temporary Foreign Worker Programme."

15 Human trafficking and human smuggling is illegal everywhere in Canada.
    For more information, see https://www.publicsafety.gc.ca/cnt/rsrcs/pblctns/
    ntnl-ctn-pln-cmbt/index-en.aspx#toc-01.1.

16 Ontario specifically prohibits recruiters from providing immigration advice. In practice, this means that immigration consultants work independently, but receive referrals from recruiters and agencies.

17 Villegas, *North of El Norte.*

18 Both Alberta (where the TFW worked) and Ontario (where the agency was headquartered) prohibit charging TFWs for jobs.

19 Eisenhardt, "Agency Theory."

20 Cundal and Seaman, "Canada's Temporary Foreign Worker Programme"; Nakache and Kinoshita, "Canadian Temporary Foreign Worker Program," 14.

21 Government of Canada, "Justice Laws Website."

22 Strauss and McGrath, "Temporary Migration"; Preibisch and Hennebry, "Buy Local, Hire Global."

23 Gesualdi-Fecteau, "Recruitment of Guatemalan Agricultural Workers."

24 Both British Columbia and Alberta require agents to be licensed. Unlicensed immigration consultants are beyond the purview of the College of Immigration and Citizenship Consultants. College of Immigration and Citizenship Consultants, "Unauthorized Practice."

25 In every province, TFWs are legally allowed to quit their jobs.

26 Gravel et al., "Embauche des travailleurs étrangers temporaires."

27 British Columbia explicitly prohibits agencies from charging fees to TFWs. Unlike other provinces, British Columbia also specifies that if employers or third parties acting on their behalf break this law then the employer can be charged under the Immigration and Refugee Protection Regulations, the Criminal Code of Canada, or the *Employment Standards Act*. They further specify that non-compliant employers can be deemed ineligible to hire foreign workers.

28 Akerlof and Shiller, *Phishing for Phools.*

29 Pouryousefi and Frooman, "Consumer Scam."

30 The Labour Market Impact Assessment (LMIA) used to be known as the Labour Market Opinion (LMO).

31 D. Brazao and R. Cribb, "Nannies Trapped in Bogus Jobs," *Toronto Star*, 14 March 2009, https://www.thestar.com/news/investigations/2009/03/14/nannies_trapped_in_bogus_jobs.html.

32 Dalton et al., "Fundamental Agency Problem."

33 See, for example, Gabriel and Macdonald, "After the International Organization for Migration."

Chapter Three

1 Bourdieu, "Forms of Capital," 248.

2 Adler and Kwon, "Social Capital."

3 Granovetter, "Strength of Weak Ties."
4 Portes, "Social Capital."
5 Preibisch and Otero, "Does Citizenship Status Matter?"
6 McLaughlin et al., "Temporary Workers, Temporary Fathers."
7 Pratt, "Circulating Sadness."
8 Rodriguez and Tiongson, "Temporary Migration Overseas."
9 In 2018, according to the OECD, the average yearly wage in Mexico was USD$16,298 and the minimum wage was 123.22 pesos (USD$5.42) per day. The average annual family income in the Philippines is PHP313,000 (or USD$6,239) according to the 2018 Family Income and Expenditure Survey published by the Philippines Statistics Authority. The daily minimum wage in the Philippines varies; it ranges from PHP243 (USD$4.60) per day for non-agricultural workers in Ilocos to PHP537 (USD$10.16) per day for non-agricultural workers in Metro Manila. In 2019, the average yearly salary in India was USD$2,020 (according to *Business Insider*) and the statutory national floor minimum wage was approximately USD$2.34 per day (according to the *Economics Times*, 25 May 2020). In 2019, the average monthly wage for non-agricultural workers in South Africa was 22,500 rand (USD$1,298.77 or USD$15,585.24 per year) according to *The South African*. Minimum wage is 20.76 rand/hour for most workers, according to the South African government. The unemployment rate was approximately 29 per cent in the second half of 2019, according to the Department of Statistics in South Africa.
   Gonzalez, "Mexico to Hike Minimum Wage"; Head, "Revealed"; McDowell, "Average Annual Income"; Organisation for Economic Co-operation and Development, "Average Wages"; Republic of the Philippines Department of Labor and Employment, *Handbook*; Republic of the Philippines Statistics Authority, "2018 Survey"; Sharma, Y.S. "A Relook at National Floor for Minimum Wages," *Economic Times*, 25 November 2020, https://economictimes.indiatimes.com/news/economy/policy/a-relook-at-national-floor-for-minimum-wages/articleshow/79396472.cms; South African Government, Department of Employment and Labour, "New National Minimum Wage"; Statistics South Africa, "Quarterly Labour Force Survey."
10 Wells et al., "Sustaining Precarious Transnational Families."
11 Carvajal Gutiérrez and Johnson, "Impact of Remittances."
12 Government of Canada, "Types of Work Permits."
13 Government of Canada, "Can My Family Come to Canada?"
14 Government of Canada, "Caregivers Will Now Have Access."
15 Government of Canada, "Facts and Figures 2017."
16 The average age of the TFWs that we interviewed was about thirty-two.
17 Foster and Taylor, "In the Shadows."

18 Ebaugh and Curry, "Fictive Kin as Social Capital"; Brasch, "Constructing Coping Strategies."

19 Portes, "Social Capital."

20 The arrangement was similar to a previous arrangement between her cousin and the TFW's mother.

21 This manager had recently discovered that the agency he had been using had charged each of his employees $1,000 to work for him, which contravenes the TFW guidelines.

22 His reluctance to use an agency stemmed in part from the fact that, when he was a TFW, an agency had fraudulently charged him $5,000 to find him a job in Canada.

23 However, even with this support, she still felt uncomfortable asking her boss about having more schedule flexibility, and he still charged her a $50 "processing fee" for her to be hired. Charging employees fees as a condition of their employment violates the Employment Standards in Ontario, where her employer is located. Her experience suggests that non-TFWs are still vulnerable to mistreatment.

24 Greenhaus and Beutell, "Conflict between Work and Family Roles."

25 Kossek and Lee, "Work-Family Conflict."

26 Lapierre et al., "Antecedents of Work-Family Enrichment."

27 Wayne et al., "Satisfaction with Work-Family Balance."

28 Shockley, Smith, and Knudsen, "Impact of Work-Life Balance."

29 Lu and Hou, "Temporary Foreign Workers."

30 Burt, *Structural Holes*; Granovetter, "Strength of Weak Ties."

Chapter Four

1 Environics Institute for Survey Research, "Focus Canada – Fall 2019."

2 Angus Reid Institute, *Immigration*, 3.

3 Finotelli and Kolb, "'The Good, the Bad and the Ugly' Reconsidered"; Akbari and MacDonald, "Immigration Policy"; Clarke, Ferrer, and Skuterud, "Labor Market Performance."

4 Interestingly, the Canadian immigration system is becoming more employer-focused, with the introduction of the provincial nominee programs which allow many TFWs to apply for permanent residency if they have steady employment in Canada. In this regard, Canadian immigration policies are becoming more like those in other countries. For an examination of the Manitoba provincial nominee program, see Carter, Morrish, and Amoyaw, "Attracting Immigrants."

5 Sweetman and Warman, "Former Temporary Foreign Workers."

6 Boyd, "Recruiting High Skill Labour."

7 Finotelli and Kolb, "'The Good, the Bad and the Ugly' Reconsidered."

8 See, for example, Underhill et al., "Migration Intermediaries"; Buckley, "From Kerala to Dubai."

9 Organisation for Economic Co-operation and Development, "International Migration Outlook," 316.

10 US Citizenship and Immigration Services, "H-1B Specialty Occupations."

11 The higher-skill TFW program, which preceded the high-wage TFW program, was more similar to the US H-1B visa in this regard.

12 US Citizenship and Immigration Services, "H-1B Specialty Occupations."

13 US Citizenship and Immigration Services, "H-2A Temporary Agricultural Workers."

14 Australian Government, Department of Home Affairs, Immigration and Citizenship. "Temporary Skill Shortage Visa."

15 Organisation for Economic Co-operation and Development, "International Migration Outlook," 238.

16 Australian Government, Department of Home Affairs, Immigration and Citizenship. "Temporary Skill Shortage Visa."

17 Australian Government, Department of Home Affairs, Immigration and Citizenship, "Seasonal Work Program Stream."

18 Australian Government, Department of Agriculture, Water and the Environment, *National Agricultural Workforce Strategy*.

19 Organisation for Economic Co-operation and Development, "International Migration Outlook," 239.

20 European Commission, EU Immigration Portal, "What Category?"

21 European Commission, EU Immigration Portal, "EU Blue Card."

22 European Union, "Work Permits."

23 Zoeteweij-Turhan, "Seasonal Workers Directive."

24 France-Visas, "Salaried Employment."

25 Republic of Portugal, Diplomatic Portal, "Type of Visas."

26 Organisation for Economic Co-operation and Development, "International Migration Outlook," 262.

27 Ibid., 264.

28 Ibid., 274.

29 Government of the Hong Kong Special Administrative Region, Immigration Department, "Imported Workers."

30 Ibid.

31 Government of the Hong Kong Special Administrative Region, Immigration Department, "Introduction of Admission Schemes."

32 Government of the Hong Kong Special Administrative Region, Immigration Department, "Introduction of Admission Schemes."

33 I use the term in-home caregiver to also refer to the live-in caregiver program.

34 HKD$4,630 is approximately USD$597.43 or CAD$788.53. Note that this is the monthly wage.

35 Government of the Hong Kong Special Administrative Region, Immigration Department, "Foreign Domestic Workers."
36 United Arab Emirates, "UAE's Policy on Domestic Helpers."
37 Ibid.
38 Ibid.
39 United Arab Emirates, "Procuring a Work Visa."
40 United Arab Emirates, "Getting a Work and Residency Permit."
41 United Arab Emirates, "Employment Contracts."
42 Uggerslev, Fassina, and Kraichy, "Recruiting Through the Stages."
43 Unfortunately, as we saw in chapter 1, TFWs in Canada are also sometimes asked to work unpaid overtime, even though this violates provincial and federal employment standards.
44 According to the OECD, the average full-time employee in South Korean worked 1,967 hours in 2019, which was higher than the average number of hours worked by Canadian employees (1,670). This number does not distinguish between different industries or occupations, but it is interesting to note that the average number of hours worked in Korea was the third highest in the world (only Mexico and Costa Rica were higher). Organisation for Economic Co-operation and Development, "Average Annual Hours."
45 Government of India, Ministry of Labour and Employment, "Draft Labour Code," Chapter III, Duties of Employer and Employee, etc., 6. Duties of Employer, (2): "Every employer shall provide and maintain, as far as is reasonably practicable, a working environment that is safe and without risk to the health of the employees," 14.
46 For more information, see the Association of Workers' Compensation Boards of Canada, "2019 Lost Time Claims in Canada," https://awcbc.org/en/statistics/#injuries.
47 The government's Labor Code states in Article 56, "Working conditions based on the principle of substantive equality between women and men may in no case be inferior to those established in this Law, and must be proportional to the importance of services and equal for the same job, without differences and / or exclusions due to ethnic origin or nationality, sex, gender, age, disability, social status, health condition, religion, opinions, sexual preferences, pregnancy, family responsibilities or marital status, except for the modalities expressly set forth in this Law." Government of Mexico, "Ley Federal del Trabajo" [Labour Code], 21, author's translation.
48 United Nations Development Program and International Labour Organization, LGBTI People and Employment, 31.
49 As an added layer of protection for this worker, I am omitting any direct quotes from our conversation.
50 Courtright, "Cronología del movimiento LGTBQ."

51 "Ministerio de Justicia y Seguridad presenta Política."
52 United Nations High Commission for Refugees. "For Salvadoran LGBTI People."
53 None of the TFWs who spoke to me told me that their passports were taken, and this is explicitly prohibited according to the TFW guidelines. However, during our outreach to possible participants, one TFW who emailed my assistant did mention that her employer had her passport and that she could not leave her place of employment (she worked in the same building as she lived). This TFW did not want to be interviewed for the book, and we put her in touch with some community organizations who could help her.
54 Binford, *Going to the Harvest*; Koo and Hanley, "Migrant Live-In Caregivers."
55 This interview was conducted in French. The transcript of this passage reads: "C'est meilleur dans les États-Unis. Les personnes qui arrivent dans les État-Unis, quand t'es maltraité dans une entreprise, qu'est-ce que tu fais? Tu changes. T'es pas obligé à rester avec cet employeur que c'est un mauvais employeur. Mais ici, t'as pas le choix, tu peux pas changer. Parce que t'es lié à un seul employeur."
56 Swider, Zimmerman, and Barrick, "Searching for the Right Fit."
57 The CRA regulations are extensive, but essentially, independent contractors are required to have considerable control over their day-to-day work (e.g., work without supervision), set their own hours, own their own tools of work, and be allowed to subcontract any tasks. This was not the case for this worker.

Chapter Five

1 According to Employment and Social Development Canada "Table 19," the total numbers of positive LMIAS issued to unique employers is as follows: 2012 = 41,975, 2013 = 35,392, 2014 = 26,017, 2015 = 16,998, 2016 = 18,933, 2017 = 21,244, 2018 = 22,382, 2019 = 31,807. Note that a positive LMIA does not necessarily mean that a work permit was issued, and the data may include overlap between years.
2 In my interviews, I spoke to company owners, franchise owners, HR managers, executives, supervisors, farmers, and managers. When I describe their experiences, I use the term "employer" or "manager" as an umbrella term to describe them all.
3 Fisher and Connelly, "Lower Cost or Just Lower Value?"
4 Sturman et al., "Is It Worth It?"
5 Binford, *Going to the Harvest*.
6 Brochu, Gross, and Worswick, "Temporary Foreign Workers and Firms."
7 Gravel et al., "Embauche des travailleurs étrangers temporaires."

8   Ibid. The study included forty participants: seventeen employers and
     twenty-three key informants from government and non-profit organizations
     (e.g., unions, employer associations, agencies).
9   Polanco, "Globalizing 'Immobile' Worksites."
10 Wright and Constantin, "Why Recruit?"
11 Gravel et al., "Embauche des travailleurs étrangers temporaires."
12 Employers' preferences for flexible labour has a long history, even when
     TFWs are not available. Most companies hire temporary agency workers,
     contractors, and direct-hire workers as well as part-time employees instead.
     See Connelly and Gallagher, "Contingent Work Research."
13 Knott, "Contentious Mobilities."
14 Fang et al., "Temporary Foreign Worker Program," 31.
15 Knott, "Contentious Mobilities."
16 According to Statistics Canada, the unemployment rates for his city were as
     follows: 2013: 9.3%; 2014: 8.2%; 2015: 8.6%; 2016: 8.4%; 2017: 6.6%; 2018:
     7%' and 2019: 7.1%. Statistics Canada, "Table 14-10-0090-01."
17 Interestingly, the owner of a repair shop in British Columbia expressed
     strong views that individuals must always take responsibility for their own
     success and well-being. He told me, "You don't have any rights. You have the
     right to suck air and make a living. Get off your ass and make a living. All of
     this rights, you know, rights of workers and rights of children and rights of
     women and rights whatever, it's all bullshit. It's just written stuff. If you look
     at the laws of nature, those designate what the rights are. And the laws of
     nature are if you don't get off your ass and make some food for today you're
     going to go hungry, and if you don't get off your ass and make some money
     so you can put a shelter over your head, you're going to be cold and wet
     tonight" (MAN08, male repair company owner in British Columbia). This
     owner believed that each individual needed to simply adapt to the current
     economic environment, and people should work independently to succeed.
     He stated that he did not believe that external circumstances ever warranted
     special consideration or assistance from the government or from others.
18 According to the TFW guidelines, this manager should have been adjusting
     his HR policies to make the available jobs more attractive to Canadians
     (e.g., higher wages, better working conditions) and improving his
     recruitment practices (e.g., targeting his job ads more effectively). The long-
     term plan should have been to gradually increase the number of returning
     Canadian seasonal employees, while reducing his reliance on the TFWs.
19 Note that I am using the term "in-home caregiver" to also refer to live-
     in caregivers.
20 This is, indeed, the purpose of the audit.

21 A granary is similar to a barn, except that it is used solely to store grain or
    animal feed (in this regard it is more similar to a silo except that it is a smaller
    structure, and more rectangular). Granaries are not insulated and they do
    not have running water. Some granaries have openings in the walls near the
    ceiling; these are not windows, but rather openings where the grain is added.
    According to the National Research Council of Canada's *National Building
    Code – 2019 Alberta Edition,* a building in which people live must have
    adequate ventilation, windows in all bedrooms unless they have sprinklers or
    a door that leads directly outside, and enough insulation so that the dwelling
    can be heated to 22°c. The entrance must have a door to the outside that locks,
    but it must also be openable from the outside without the use of keys, tools, or
    special knowledge and without the removal of sashes or hardware.
22 Government of Canada, "Employers Found Non-Compliant."
23 Unfortunately, more general human resource management and
    organizational behaviour research conducted on non-tfws may not be
    helpful in this regard because leadership theories such as abusive supervision
    do not account for the severity of the mistreatment that legal migrant
    workers experience. tfws certainly experience "hostile verbal and nonverbal
    behavior" from their managers, but the employers who mistreat tfws often
    go beyond this and engage in behaviour that is fraudulent.

Chapter Six

1   Cedillo, Lippel, and Nakache, "Health and Safety of Temporary
    Foreign Workers."
2   Canadian Chamber of Commerce, "Response to the Consultation."
3   Note that I am using the term "in-home caregiver" to also refer to live-
    in caregivers.
4   Canadian Federation of Independent Business, "Time to Take the 'Temporary'
    Out"; Restaurants Canada, "Changes Coming"; Hotel Association of Canada.
    "Written Submission."
5   Government of Canada, "Agri-Food Pilot."
6   Government of Canada, "Atlantic Immigration Program."
7   Migrant Rights Network, "Migrants Mandate Letter."
8   Statistics Canada, "Introduction to the National Occupational Classification."
9   Restaurants Canada, "Pushing for a Better tfwp."
10 Employers of high-wage tfws are not required to provide housing or
    accommodations to these employees.
11 W. Stueck, "B.C.'s $10-million Quarantine Program seen as Model for how to
    treat Farm Workers in Pandemic," *Globe and Mail,* 15 July 2020, https://www.

theglobeandmail.com/canada/british-columbia/article-bc-seen-as-model-for-how-to-treat-migrant-workers/; C. Wilson, "Province to Cover Isolation Costs for Foreign Workers hired by B.C. Farms," *Times Colonist*, 12 December 2020, https://www.timescolonist.com/business/province-to-cover-isolation-costs-for-foreign-workers-hired-by-bc-farms-4686205.

12 K. Blaze Baum and T. Grant, "Mayors, Health Officials urge Ontario to Manage Quarantine Period for Migrant Farm Workers," *Globe and Mail*, 15 July 2020, https://www.theglobeandmail.com/canada/article-mayors-health-officials-urge-ontario-to-manage-quarantine-period-for/; T. Grant and K. Blaze Baum, "Ottawa Vows Crackdown on Employers Violating Health Protection Rules for Migrant Farm Workers," *Globe and Mail*, 22 June 2020, https://www.theglobeandmail.com/canada/article-ottawa-vows-crackdown-on-employers-violating-health-protection-rules/.

13 Bonifacio Eugenio Romero, 31; Rogelio Muñoz Santos, 24; and Juan Lopez Chaparro, 55; all from Mexico.

14 K. Blaze Baum and T. Grant, "Essential but Expendable: How Canada Failed Migrant Farm Workers," *Globe and Mail*, 16 June 2020, https://www.theglobeandmail.com/canada/article-essential-but-expendable-how-canada-failed-migrant-farm-workers/.

15 T. Grant and K. Blaze Baum, "Migrant Workers on Farms across Canada Are Being Told They Can't Leave, Raising Rights Concerns," *Globe and Mail*, 3 August 2020, https://www.theglobeandmail.com/business/article-migrant-workers-on-farms-across-canada-are-being-told-they-cant-leave/; Weikle, "COVID Outbreaks on Farms."

16 Kelley, Wirsig, and Smart, "Bitter Harvest."

17 T. Grant, "Ban on Temporary Foreign Workers in New Brunswick Pressures Food Producers," *Globe and Mail*, 18 May 2020, https://www.theglobeandmail.com/business/article-ban-on-temporary-foreign-workers-in-new-brunswick-pressures-food/.

18 Vernon, "Alberta Push to Suspend TFW Program."

19 T. Grant, "Canada's Food Supply at Risk as Pandemic Tightens Borders to Farm Workers," *Globe and Mail*, 1 April 2020, https://www.theglobeandmail.com/business/article-canadas-food-supply-at-risk-as-pandemic-tightens-borders-to-farm/; A. Stephenson, "TFW Shortage Will Cause Headaches for Agriculture Sector: Report," *Calgary Herald*, 14 July 2020, https://calgaryherald.com/business/local-business/tfw-shortage-will-cause-headaches-for-agriculture-sector-report.

20 For more on this, see Hennebry and Preibisch, "Model for Managed Migration?"

21 Stueck, "B.C.'s $10-million Quarantine Program."

Bibliography

Newspapers

Calgary Herald

Economic Times

Globe and Mail

Times Colonist (Victoria, BC)

Toronto Star

Vancouver Sun

Other Works

Adler, P.S., and S.-W. Kwon. "Social Capital: Prospects for a New Concept." *Academy of Management Review* 27, no. 1 (2002): 17–40.

Akbari, A.H., and M. MacDonald. "Immigration Policy in Australia, Canada, New Zealand, and the United States: An Overview of Recent Trends." *International Migration Review* 48, no. 3 (2014): 801–22.

Akerlof, G.A., and R.J. Shiller. *Phishing for Phools: The Economics of Manipulation and Deception.* Princeton, NJ: Princeton University Press, 2015.

Akhtar, F., M. Schwandt, L. Hanson, A. Stevens, and S. Tucker. "Health Wanted: Social Determinants of Health among Migrant Workers in Saskatchewan." Working Paper, May 2018. http://migrantwork.ca/wp-content/uploads/2018/05/Health-Wanted-Working-Paper-May-14-2018.pdf.

André, I. "The Genesis and Persistence of the Commonwealth Caribbean Seasonal Agricultural Workers Program in Canada." *Osgoode Hall Law Journal* 28, no. 2 (1990): 243–301.

Angus Reid Institute. *Immigration: Half Back Current Targets, but Colossal Misperceptions, Pushback over Refugees, Cloud Debate.* 7 October 2019. http://angusreid.org/wp-content/uploads/2019/10/2019.10.04_Immigration-Views.pdf.

Australian Government, Department of Agriculture, Water and the Environment. *National Agricultural Workforce Strategy Literature Review.*

Canberra: Department of Agriculture, Water and the Environment, 2020. https://haveyoursay.awe.gov.au/53281/widgets/276752/documents/136878.

– Department of Home Affairs, Immigration and Citizenship. "Seasonal Work Program Stream." Accessed 20 November 2020. https://immi. homeaffairs.gov.au/visas/getting-a-visa/visa-listing/temporary-work-403/ seasonal-worker-program.

– "Temporary Skill Shortage Visa." Accessed 20 November 2020. https:// immi.homeaffairs.gov.au/visas/getting-a-visa/visa-listing/temporary-skill-shortage-482.

Bakan, A.B., and D. Stasiulis. "Foreign Domestic Worker Policy in Canada and the Social Boundaries of Modern Citizenship." In *Not One of the Family*, edited by A.B. Bakan and D. Stasiulis, 29–52. Toronto: University of Toronto Press, 1997.

– , eds. *Not One of the Family*. Toronto: University of Toronto Press, 1997.

Barber, M. "Domestic Service (Caregiving) in Canada." *The Canadian Encyclopedia*, 7 February 2006. https://www.thecanadianencyclopedia.ca/ en/article/domestic-service.

Barnes, C.M., L. Lucianetti, D.P. Bhave, and M.S. Christian. "'You Wouldn't Like Me when I'm Sleepy': Leaders' Sleep, Daily Abusive Supervision, and Work Unit Engagement." *Academy of Management Journal* 58, no. 5 (2015): 1419–37.

Binford, L. *Tomorrow We're All Going to the Harvest: Temporary Foreign Worker Programs and Neoliberal Political Economy*. Austin: University of Texas Press, 2013.

Binford, L., and K. Preibisch. "Interrogating Racialized Global Labor Supply: Caribbean and Mexican Workers in Canada's SAWP." In *Tomorrow We're All Going to the Harvest: Temporary Foreign Worker Programs and Neoliberal Political Economy*, by L. Binford, 93–115. Austin: University of Texas Press, 2013.

Boucher, A. "Measuring Migrant Worker Rights Violations in Practice: The Example of Temporary Skilled Visas in Australia." *Journal of Industrial Relations* 61, no. 2 (2019): 277–301.

Bourdieu, P. "The Forms of Capital." In *Handbook of Theory and Research for the Sociology of Education*, edited by J.G. Richardson, 241–58. New York: Greenwood, 1986.

Boyd, M. "Recruiting High Skill Labour in North America: Policies, Outcomes and Futures." *International Migration* 52, no. 3 (2014): 40–54.

Brasch, K. "Constructing Coping Strategies: Migrants Seeking Stability in Social Networks." In *Producing and Negotiating Non-Citizenship: Precarious Legal Status in Canada*, edited by L. Goldring and P. Landolt, 118–36. Toronto: University of Toronto Press, 2013.

Brochu, P., T. Gross, and C. Worswick. "Temporary Foreign Workers and Firms: Theory and Canadian Evidence." *Canadian Journal of Economics* 53, no. 3 (2020): 871–915.

Buckley, M. "From Kerala to Dubai and Back Again: Construction Migrants and the Global Economic Crisis." *Geoforum* 43, no. 2 (2012): 250–9.

Burt, R.S. *Structural Holes: The Social Structure of Competition.* Cambridge, MA: Harvard University Press, 1995.

Byrne, A., A.M. Dioniso, J. Barling, A. Akers, J. Robertson, R. Lys, J. Wylie, and K. Dupré. "The Depleted Leader: The Influence of Leaders' Diminished Psychological Resources on Leadership Behaviors." *Leadership Quarterly* 25, no. 2 (2014): 344–57.

Canadian Centre for Occupational Health and Safety. "OH&S Legislation in Canada –Three Rights of Workers." Government of Canada. Accessed 11 December 2019. https://www.ccohs.ca/oshanswers/legisl/three_rights.html.

Canadian Chamber of Commerce. "Response to the Government of Canada / IRCC's Consultation on Introducing Occupation-specific Work Permits under the Temporary Foreign Worker Program." 22 July 2019. https://www.whistlerchamber.com/wp-content/uploads/2019/08/2019-07-22_CanadianChamber_TFW-OccupSpecPermitsConsultation.pdf.

Canadian Council for Refugees. "Evaluating Migrant Workers Rights in Canada 2018." Montreal: CCR, 2018. https://ccrweb.ca/sites/ccrweb.ca/files/reportcards_complete_en.pdf.

Canadian Federation of Independent Business. "Time to Take the 'Temporary' Out of the Temporary Foreign Worker Program." News release, 18 May 2016. https://www.cfib-fcei.ca/en/media/cfib-proposes-path-permanent-residency-replace-temporary-foreign-worker-program.

Carter, T., M. Morrish, and B. Amoyaw. "Attracting Immigrants to Smaller Urban and Rural Communities: Lessons Learned from the Manitoba Provincial Nominee Program." *International Migration and Integration* 9, no. 2 (2008): 161–83.

Carvajal Gutiérrez, L., and T.G. Johnson. "The Impact of Remittances from Canada's Seasonal Workers Programme on Mexican Farms." *International Labor Review* 155, no. 2 (2016): 297–314.

Cedillo, L., K. Lippel, and D. Nakache. "Factors Influencing the Health and Safety of Temporary Foreign Workers in Skilled and Low-Skilled Occupations in Canada." *New Solutions: A Journal of Environmental and Occupational Health and Safety* 29, no. 3 (2019): 422–58.

Clarke, A., A. Ferrer, and M. Skuterud. "A Comparative Analysis of the Labor Market Performance of University-Educated Immigrants in Australia,

Canada, and the United States: Does Policy Matter?" *Journal of Labor Economics* 37, no. S2 (2019): S443–90.

College of Immigration and Citizenship Consultants. "Unauthorized Practice." Accessed 19 July 2022. https://college-ic.ca/protecting-the-public/unauthorized-practice.

Connelly, C.E., and D.G. Gallagher. "Emerging Trends in Contingent Work Research." *Journal of Management* 30, no. 6 (2004): 959–83.

Courtright, N.C. "La cronología del movimiento LGTBQ en San Salvador" [The Chronology of the LGTBQ Movement in San Salvador]. Factum. 24 June 2016. https://www.revistafactum.com/la-cronologia-del-movimiento-lgtb-salvador/.

Cundal, K., and B. Seaman. "Canada's Temporary Foreign Worker Programme: A Discussion of Human Rights Issues." *Migration Letters* 9, no. 3 (2012): 201–14.

Dalton, D.R., M.A. Hitt, S.T. Certo, and C.M. Dalton. "The Fundamental Agency Problem and Its Mitigation: Independence, Equity, and the Market for Corporate Control." *The Academy of Management Annals* 1, no. 1 (2007): 1–64.

Ebaugh, H.R., and M. Curry. "Fictive Kin as Social Capital in New Immigrant Communities." *Sociological Perspectives* 43, no. 2 (2000): 189–209.

Eisenhardt, K.M. "Agency Theory: An Assessment and Review." *Academy of Management Review* 14, no. 1 (1989): 57–74.

Employment and Social Development Canada. "Labour Market Impact Assessment Application High-Wage Positions." ESDC EMP5626. Accessed 8 August 2019. https://catalogue.servicecanada.gc.ca/content/EForms/en/Detail.html?Form=EMP5626.

– "Labour Market Impact Assessment Application In-Home Caregiver Positions." EMP5628. Accessed 11 December 2019. https://catalogue.servicecanada.gc.ca/content/EForms/en/Detail.html?Form=EMP5628.

– "Labour Market Impact Assessment Application Low-Wage Positions." EMP5627. Accessed 3 August 2019. https://catalogue.servicecanada.gc.ca/content/EForms/en/Detail.html?Form=EMP5627.

– "Labour Market Impact Assessment Application Seasonal Agricultural Worker Program." EMP5389. Accessed 2 August 2019. https://catalogue.servicecanada.gc.ca/content/EForms/en/Detail.html?Form=EMP5389.

– "Table 19: Number of unique employers who received a positive Labour Market Impact Assessments (LMIA) by stream and province/territory between 2012 and 2019" (Record ID 76defa14-473e-41e2-abfa-60021c4d934b) [Data set]. Accessed 16 December 2020. https://open.canada.ca/data/en/dataset/76defa14-473e-41e2-abfa-60021c4d934b.

Environics Institute for Survey Research. "Focus Canada – Fall 2019: Canadian Public Opinion About Immigration and Refugees: Final Report." 25 November 2019. https://www.environicsinstitute.org/docs/default-source/ project-documents/focus-canada-fall-2019—immigration-refugees/focus-canada-fall-2019-survey-on-immigration-and-refugees—final-report.pdf.

European Commission, EU Immigration Portal. "EU Blue Card Essential Information." Accessed 20 November 2020. https://ec.europa.eu/ immigration/blue-card/essential-information_en.

– "What Category Do I Fit Into?" Accessed 20 November 2020. https:// ec.europa.eu/immigration/general-information/what-category-do-i-fit_en.

European Union. "Work Permits." Accessed 20 November 2020. https:// europa.eu/youreurope/citizens/work/work-abroad/work-permits/index_ en.htm.

Fang, T., H. Sapeha, K. Neil, G. Williams, O. Jaunty-Aidamenbor, and T. Osmond. "The Temporary Foreign Worker Program and Employers in Labrador." St. John's, NL: The Leslie Harris Centre for Regional Policy and Development, Memorial University, 2017. https://research.library.mun. ca/12792/1/TFWs_-_Report_Final_2017-04-10.pdf.

Finotelli, C., and H. Kolb. "'The Good, the Bad and the Ugly' Reconsidered: A Comparison of German, Canadian and Spanish Labour Migration Policies." *Journal of Comparative Policy Analysis* 19, no. 1 (2017): 72–86.

Fisher S.L., and C.E. Connelly. "Lower Cost or Just Lower Value? Modeling the Organizational Costs and Benefits of Contingent Work." *Academy of Management Discoveries* 3, no. 2 (2017): 165–186.

Foster, J., and A. Taylor. "In the Shadows: Exploring the Notion of 'Community' for Temporary Foreign Workers in a Boomtown." *Canadian Journal of Sociology* 38, no. 2 (2013): 167–89.

France-Visas. "Salaried Employment." Accessed 20 November 2020. https:// france-visas.gouv.fr/en_US/web/france-visas/salaried-employment.

Fudge, J. "Global Care Chains, Employment Agencies, and the Conundrum of Jurisdiction: Decent Work for Domestic Workers in Canada." *Canadian Journal of Women and the Law* 23, no. 1 (2011): 235–64.

Fudge, J., and F. MacPhail. "The Temporary Foreign Worker Program in Canada: Low-Skilled Workers as an Extreme Form of Flexible Labor." *Comparative Labor Law and Policy* 31 (2009): 5–45.

Fudge, J., and J.-C. Tham. "Dishing Up Migrant Workers for the Canadian Food Services Sector: Labor Law and the Demand for Migrant Workers." *Comparative Labor Law and Policy* 39 (2017): 1–27.

Gabriel, C., and L. Macdonald. "After the International Organization for Migration: Recruitment of Guatemalan Temporary Agricultural Workers

to Canada." *Journal of Ethnic and Migration Studies* 44, no. 10 (2018):
1706–24.

Gesualdi-Fecteau, D. "The Recruitment of Guatemalan Agricultural Workers
by Canadian Employers: Mapping the Web of a Transnational Network."
International Journal of Migration and Border Studies 1, no. 3 (2014): 291–302.

Gonzalez, A. "Mexico to Hike Daily Minimum Wage by 20%, Experts Worry
about Inflation." Reuters, 16 December 2019. https://www.reuters.com/
article/us-mexico-wages/mexico-to-hike-daily-minimum-wage-by-20-
experts-worry-about-inflation-idUSKBN1YL051.

Government of Canada. "2018 Annual Report to Parliament on
Immigration." Accessed 11 December 2019. https://www.canada.ca/
en/immigration-refugees-citizenship/corporate/publications-manuals/
annual-report-parliament-immigration-2018/report.html.

– "Agri-Food Pilot: About the Pilot." Accessed 14 January 2022. https://www.
canada.ca/en/immigration-refugees-citizenship/services/immigrate-canada/
agri-food-pilot/about.html.

– "Atlantic Immigration Program." Accessed 14 January 2022. https://www.
canada.ca/en/immigration-refugees-citizenship/services/immigrate-canada/
atlantic-immigration-pilot.html.

– "Can My Family Come to Canada with Me if I Am a Live-in Caregiver?"
Accessed 11 December 2019. https://www.cic.gc.ca/english/helpcentre/
answer.asp?qnum=241&top=28.

– "Caregivers Will Now Have Access to New Pathways to Permanent
Residence." Accessed 11 December 2019. https://www.canada.ca/en/
immigration-refugees-citizenship/news/2019/02/caregivers-will-now-have-
access-to-new-pathways-to-permanent-residence.html.

– "Code of Professional Conduct for College of Immigration and
Citizenship Consultants Licensees: SOR/2022-128 – Canada Gazette,
Part II, Volume 156, Number 13." Accessed 18 October 2022. https://
www.gazette.gc.ca/rp-pr/p2/2022/2022-06-22/html/sor-dors128-eng.html.

– "Employers Who Have Been Found Non-Compliant." Accessed 11
November 2020. https://www.canada.ca/en/immigration-refugees-
citizenship/services/work-canada/employers-non-compliant.html.

– "Facts and Figures 2017 – Immigration Overview – Temporary Residents."
https://open.canada.ca/data/en/dataset/2bf9f856-20fe-4644-bf74-
c8e45b3d94bd.

– "Hire a Temporary Foreign Worker in a High-Wage or Low-Wage Position."
Accessed 11 December 2019. https://www.canada.ca/en/employment-
social-development/services/foreign-workers/median-wage.html.

– "Hire a Temporary Worker as an In-home Caregiver: Program
Requirements." Accessed 11 December 2019. https://www.canada.ca/

en/employment-social-development/services/foreign-workers/caregiver/
requirements.html.
– "Hire a Temporary Worker as an In-home Caregiver: Wages, Working
Conditions and Occupations." Accessed 11 December 2019. https://www.
canada.ca/en/employment-social-development/services/foreign-workers/
caregiver/working-conditions.html.
– "Hire a Temporary Worker through the Seasonal Agricultural Worker ·
Program: Overview." Accessed 11 December 2019. https://www.canada.ca/
en/employment-social-development/services/foreign-workers/agricultural/
seasonal-agricultural.html.
– "Hire a Temporary Worker through the Seasonal Agricultural Worker
Program: Program Requirements." Accessed 11 December 2019. https://
www.canada.ca/en/employment-social-development/services/foreign-
workers/agricultural/seasonal-agricultural/requirements.html.
– "Justice Laws Website – Immigration and Refugee Protection Act
(S.C. 2001, c. 27)." Accessed 19 July 2022. https://laws-lois.justice.gc.ca/eng/
acts/i-2.5/section-91.html.
– "Live-in Caregiver Program: Who Is Eligible." Accessed 11 December 2019.
https://www.canada.ca/en/immigration-refugees-citizenship/services/work-
canada/hire-foreign-worker/caregiver-program/hire-caregiver.html.
– "Occupational Health and Safety in Federally Regulated Workplaces."
Accessed 11 December 2019. https://www.canada.ca/en/employment-
social-development/services/health-safety/workplace-safety.html.
– "Refusal to Process a Labour Market Impact Assessment Application."
Accessed 11 December 2019. https://www.canada.ca/en/employment-
social-development/services/foreign-workers/refusal.html.
– "Types of Work Permits for Your Situation." Accessed 11 December 2019.
https://www.cic.gc.ca/english/work/apply-who-permit-result.asp?q1_
options=1i&q2_options=2d.
Government of India, Ministry of Labour and Employment. "The Draft
Labour Code on Occupational Safety, Health and Working Conditions."
23 April 2018. https://labour.gov.in/sites/default/files/Last_Date_Extended_
for_OSH_Code_0.pdf.
Government of Mexico. "Ley federal del trabajo, Última reforma DOF 18-05-
2022" [Labour Code], 2019. https://www.diputados.gob.mx/LeyesBiblio/
pdf/LFT.pdf.
Government of the Hong Kong Special Administrative Region, Immigration
Department. "Foreign Domestic Workers." Accessed 20 November 2020.
https://www.immd.gov.hk/eng/services/visas/foreign_domestic_helpers.html.
– "Imported Workers." Accessed 20 November 2020. https://www.immd.gov.
hk/eng/services/visas/imported_worker.html.

– "Introduction of Admission Schemes for Talent, Professionals and Entrepreneurs." Accessed 20 November 2020. https://www.immd.gov.hk/eng/useful_information/admission-schemes-talents-professionals-entrepreneurs.html#gep_pro.

Granovetter, M.S. "The Strength of Weak Ties." *American Journal of Sociology* 78, no. 6 (1973): 1360–80.

Gravel, S., S. Bernstein, F. Villanueva, J. Hanley, D. Crespo-Villarreal, and E. Ostiguy. "Le recours à l'embauche des travailleurs étrangers temporaires dans les secteurs saisonniers au Québec: Le point de vue des employeurs." *Canadian Ethnic Studies* 49, no. 2 (2017): 75–98.

Greenhaus, J.H., and N.J. Beutell. "Sources of Conflict between Work and Family Roles." *Academy of Management Review* 10, no. 1 (1985): 76–88.

Gross, D.M. "Conditions for an Efficient Canadian Temporary Foreign Worker Program: The Case of Quebec." *Canadian Ethnic Studies* 49, no. 2 (2017): 99–119.

Head, T. "Revealed: The Average Salary Earned in South Africa – It's Gone Up." *The South African*, 5 April 2020. https://www.thesouthafrican.com/news/finance/average-wage-in-south-africa-2020-how-much/.

Hennebry, J.L., and K. Preibisch, "A Model for Managed Migration? Re-examining Best Practices in Canada's Seasonal Agricultural Worker Program." *International Migration* 50, no. S1 (2010): e19–40.

Hotel Association of Canada. "Written Submission for the Pre-budget Consultations in Advance of the 2020 Budget." August 2019. http://www.hotelassociation.ca/wp-content/uploads/2019/08/HAC-Pre-Budget-2020-Submission-Final.pdf.

Immigration, Refugees and Citizenship Canada. "Facts and Figures 2016: Immigration Overview – Temporary Residents." 2016. https://www.cic.gc.ca/opendata-donneesouvertes/data/Facts_and_Figures_2016_TR_EN.pdf.

Jensen, M.C., and W.H. Meckling. "Theory of the Firm: Managerial Behavior, Agency Costs and Ownership Structure." *Journal of Financial Economics* 3, no. 4 (1976): 305–60.

Kelley, M., K. Wirsig, and V. Smart. "Bitter Harvest." CBC *News*, 29 November 2020. https://newsinteractives.cbc.ca/longform/bitter-harvest-migrant-workers-pandemic.

Knott, C. "Contentious Mobilities and Cheap(er) Labour: Temporary Foreign Workers in a New Brunswick Seafood Processing Community." *Canadian Journal of Sociology* 41, no. 3 (2016): 375–97.

Koo, J.-H., and J. Hanley. "Migrant Live-In Caregivers: Control, Consensus, and Resistance in the Workplace and the Community." In *Unfree Labour?*

Struggles of Migrant and Immigrant Workers in Canada, edited by A. Choudry and A.A. Smith, 37–54. Oakland, CA: PM Press, 2016.

Kossek, E.E., and K.H. Lee. "Work-Family Conflict and Work-Life Conflict." *Oxford Research Encyclopedia of Business and Management*. Oxford University Press, 26 October 2017. https://oxfordre.com/business/view/10.1093/acrefore/9780190224851.001.0001/acrefore-9780190224851-e-52.

Lapierre, L.M., Y. Li, H.K. Kwan, J.H. Greenhaus, M.S. DiRenzo, and P. Shao. "A Meta-Analysis of the Antecedents of Work-Family Enrichment." *Journal of Organizational Behavior* 39, no. 4 (2018): 385–401.

Lenard, P.T., and C. Straehle, eds. *Legislated Inequality: Temporary Labour Migration in Canada*. Montreal: McGill-Queen's University Press, 2012.

Leo, G. "Waitresses in Saskatchewan Lose Jobs to Foreign Workers: Long-Term Employees Fired and Heartbroken. CBC News, 18 April 2014. https://www.cbc.ca/news/canada/saskatchewan/waitresses-in-saskatchewan-lose-jobs-to-foreign-workers-1.2615157.

Lu, Y., and F. Hou. "Temporary Foreign Workers in the Canadian Labour Force: Open Versus Employer-Specific Work Permits." Catalogue No. 11-626-X-2019016 – No. 102. Ottawa: Statistics Canada, 2019. https://www150.statcan.gc.ca/n1/en/pub/11-626-x/11-626-x2019016-eng.pdf?st=sP84iYJi

Mackey, J.D., B. Parker Ellen III, C.P. McAllister, and K.C. Alexander. "The Dark Side of Leadership: A Systematic Literature Review and Meta-Analysis of Destructive Leadership Research." *Journal of Business Research* 132 (2021): 705–18.

McDowell, E. "Here's the Average Annual Income in 25 Countries, Ranked from Lowest to Highest." *Business Insider*, 7 August 2019. https://www.businessinsider.com/average-annual-income-around-the-world-2019-8#24-india-2.

McLaughlin, J., J. Hennebry, and T. Haines. "Paper versus Practice: Occupational Health and Safety Protections and Realities for Temporary Foreign Agricultural Workers in Ontario." *PISTES: Perspectives interdisciplinaires sur le travail et la santé* 16, no. 2 (2014): 1–20.

McLaughlin, J., D. Wells, A. Díaz Mendiburo, A. Lyn, and B. Vasilevska. "Temporary Workers, Temporary Fathers: Transnational Family Impacts of Canada's Seasonal Agricultural Worker Program." *Relations Industrielles / Industrial Relations* 72, no. 4 (2017): 682–709.

Migrant Rights Network. "Migrants Mandate Letter to Federal Cabinet." 29 October 2021. https://migrantrights.ca/migrants-mandate-letter-to-federal-cabinet/.

"Ministerio de Justicia y Seguridad presenta política para la atención a la población LGBTI" [Ministry of Justice and Security Presents a Policy for the

LGBTI Population]. Diversidad Sexual. 16 April 2018. http://inclusionsocial.
egob.sv/ministerio-de-justicia-y-seguridad-presenta-politica-para-la-
atencion-a-la-poblacion-lgbti/.

Nakache, D., and P. Kinoshita. "The Canadian Temporary Foreign Worker
Program: Do Short-Term Economic Needs Prevail over Human Rights
Concerns?" IRPP Study, No. 5 (May 2010). https://papers.ssrn.com/sol3/
papers.cfm?abstract_id=1617255.

National Research Council of Canada. National Building Code – 2019 Alberta
Edition. Ottawa: NRCC, 2019. https://nrc-publications.canada.ca/eng/view/
ft/?id=3e93ecc7-7ad6-43ff-ac1e-89c0d033b8aa.

Organisation for Economic Co-operation and Development. "Average
Annual Hours Actually Worked per Worker." Accessed 20 November 2020.
https://stats.oecd.org/Index.aspx?DataSetCode=ANhrS.

– "Average Wages – Total, US Dollars, 2018." Accessed 22 December 2020.
https://data.oecd.org/earnwage/average-wages.htm.

– "International Migration Outlook 2021." Accessed 15 December 2021.
https://www.oecd.org/migration/international-migration-outlook-
1999124x.htm.

Oxman-Martinez, J., J. Hanley, and L. Cheung. "Another Look at the Live-in
Caregivers Program: An Analysis of an Action Research Survey Conducted
by PINAY, the Quebec Filipino Women's Association with the Centre for
Applied Family Studies." Montreal: Centre de recherche interuniversitaire
de Montréal sur l'immigration, l'intégration et la dynamique urbaine,
no. 24, 2004. http://s3.amazonaws.com/migrants_heroku_production/
datas/198/Oxman-Martinez_Hanley_Cheung_2004_original.
pdf?1312424790.

Pfeffer, A. "Rise in Foreign Temp Workers Questioned by Labour Groups."
CBC News, 10 April 2013. https://www.cbc.ca/news/politics/rise-in-foreign-
temp-workers-questioned-by-labour-groups-1.1361027.

Polanco, G. "Globalizing 'Immobile' Worksites: Fast Food under Canada's
Temporary Foreign Worker Program." In Unfree Labour: Struggles of Migrant
and Immigrant Workers in Canada, edited by A. Choudry and A.A. Smith,
71–86. Oakland, CA: PM Press, 2016.

Portes, A. "Social Capital: Its Origins and Applications in Modern Sociology."
Annual Review of Sociology 24, no. 1 (1998): 1–24.

Portugal, Republic of, Diplomatic Portal. "Type of Visas." Accessed 20
November 2020. https://www.vistos.mne.pt/en/short-stay-visas-schengen/
general-information/type-of-visas#seasonal-work-visa.

Pouryousefi, S., and J. Frooman. "The Consumer Scam: An Agency-Theoretic
Approach." Journal of Business Ethics 154, no. 1 (2019): 1–12.

Pratt, G. "Circulating Sadness: Witnessing Filipina Mothers' Stories of Family Separation." *Gender, Place & Culture* 16, no. 1 (2009): 3–22.

Preibisch, K., and J. Hennebry. "Buy Local, Hire Global: Temporary Migration in Canadian Agriculture." In *Legislated Inequality: Temporary Labour Migration in Canada*, edited by P.T. Lenard and C. Straehle, 48–72. Montreal: McGill-Queen's University Press, 2012.

Preibisch, K., and G. Otero. "Does Citizenship Status Matter in Canadian Agriculture? Workplace Health and Safety for Migrant and Immigrant Laborers." *Rural Sociology* 79, no. 2 (2014): 174–99.

Prokopenko, E., and F. Hou. "How Temporary Were Canada's Temporary Foreign Workers?" Catalogue No. 11F0019M – No. 402. Ottawa: Statistics Canada, 2018. https://www150.statcan.gc.ca/n1/pub/11f0019m/11f0019m2018402-eng.htm.

Republic of the Philippine Statistics Authority. "2018 Family Income and Expenditure Survey: Volume 1 – National and Regional Estimates." Accessed 22 December 2020. https://psa.gov.ph/sites/default/files/FIES%20 2018%20Final%20Report.pdf.

Restaurants Canada. "Changes Coming to Atlantic Immigration Pilot." 20 March 2019. https://www.restaurantscanada.org/industry-news/changes-coming-to-atlantic-immigration-pilot/.

– "Pushing for a Better TFWP." 10 December 2014. https://www.restaurantscanada.org/industry-news/pushing-for-a-better-tfwp/.

– "TFW Program Changes Cap Calculation." 26 September 2019. https://www.restaurantscanada.org/industry-news/tfw-program-changes-cap-calculation/.

Robillard, C., J. McLaughlin, D.C. Cole, B. Vasilevska, and R. Gendron. "'Caught in the Same Webs' – Service Providers' Insights on Gender-Based and Structural Violence among Female Temporary Foreign Workers in Canada." *International Migration and Integration* 19, no. 3 (2018): 583–606.

Rodriguez, E.R., and E.R. Tiongson. "Temporary Migration Overseas and Household Labor Supply: Evidence from Urban Philippines." *International Migration Review* 35, no. 3 (2001): 709–25.

Shockley, K.M., C.R. Smith, and E.A. Knudsen. "The Impact of Work-Life Balance on Employee Retention." In *The Wiley Blackwell Handbook of the Psychology of Recruitment, Selection and Employee Retention*, edited by H.W. Goldstein, E.D. Pulakos, C. Semedo, and J. Passmore, 513–43. New York: John Wiley & Sons, 2017.

Skrivankova, K. *Between Decent Work and Forced Labour: Examining the Continuum of Exploitation*. York, England: Joseph Rowntree Foundation, 2010.

South African Government, Department of Employment and Labour. "Employment and Labour on New National Minimum Wage Rate." Media release. 24 February 2020. https://www.gov.za/speeches/new-nmw-base-rate-come-effect-march-%E2%80%93-department-employment-and-labour-24-feb-2020-0000#:~:text=The%20new%20rate%20for%20the,applicable%2-0on%2001%20March%202020.

Statistics Canada. "Introduction to the National Occupational Classification (NOC) 2021 Version 1.0." Accessed 14 January 2022. https://www.statcan.gc.ca/en/subjects/standard/noc/2021/introductionV1.

– *Table 14-10-0090-01 Labour Force Characteristics by Province, Territory and Economic Region, Annual: Saint John-St. Stephen, New Brunswick* [Data Set]. 8 January 2021. https://www150.statcan.gc.ca/t1/tbl1/en/tv.action?pid=1410009001.

Statistics South Africa. "Quarterly Labour Force Survey (QLFS) – Q4:2019." Media release, 11 February 2020. http://www.statssa.gov.za/?p=12948.

Strauss, K., and S. McGrath. "Temporary Migration, Precarious Employment and Unfree Labour Relations: Exploring the 'Continuum of Exploitation' in Canada's Temporary Foreign Worker Program." *Geoforum* 78 (2017): 199–208.

Sturman, M.C., C.O. Trevor, J.W. Boudreau, and B. Gerhart. "Is It Worth It to Win the Talent War? Evaluating the Utility of Performance-Based Pay." *Personnel Psychology* 56, no. 4 (2003): 997–1035.

Sweetman, A., and C. Warman. "Former Temporary Foreign Workers and International Students as Sources of Permanent Immigration." *Canadian Public Policy* 40, no. 4 (2014): 391–407.

Swider, B.W., R.D. Zimmerman, and M.R. Barrick. "Searching for the Right Fit: Development of Applicant Person-Organization Fit Perceptions during the Recruitment Process." *Journal of Applied Psychology* 100, no. 3 (2015): 880–93.

Uggerslev, K.L., N.E. Fassina, and D. Kraichy. "Recruiting Through the Stages: A Meta-Analytic Test of Predictors of Applicant Attraction at Different Stages of the Recruiting Process." *Personnel Psychology* 65, no. 3 (2012): 597–660.

Underhill, E., D. Groutsis, D. van den Broek, and M. Rimmer. "Migration Intermediaries and Codes of Conduct: Temporary Migrant Workers in Australian Horticulture." *Journal of Business Ethics* 153, no. 3 (2018): 675–89.

United Arab Emirates. "Employment Contracts: Duration and Models in the Private Sector." https://u.ae/en/information-and-services/jobs/employment-contracts-duration-and-models-in-the-private-sector.

– "Getting a Work and Residency Permit." Accessed 20 November 2020. https://u.ae/en/information-and-services/visa-and-emirates-id/residence-visa/getting-a-work-and-residency-permit.

– "Procuring a Work Visa." Accessed 20 November 2020. https://u.ae/en/information-and-services/visa-and-emirates-id/residence-visa/getting-a-work-and-residency-permit/procuring-a-work-visa.

– "The UAE's Policy on Domestic Helpers." Accessed 20 November 2020. https://u.ae/en/information-and-services/jobs/domestic-workers/uae-policy-on-domestic-helpers.

United Nations Development Program and International Labour Organization. LGBTI *People and Employment: Discrimination Based on Sexual Orientation, Gender Identity and Expression, and Sex Characteristics in China, the Philippines and Thailand*. Bangkok: UNDP, 2018. https://www.asia-pacific.undp.org/content/rbap/en/home/library/democratic_governance/hiv_aids/lgbti-people-and-employment--discrimination-based-on-sexual-orie.html.

United Nations High Commission for Refugees (UNHCR). "For Salvadoran LGBTI People, 'At the Moment, It's Riskier than Ever.'" 26 June 2020. https://www.unhcr.org/news/stories/2020/6/5ef61ac94/salvadoran-lgbti-people-moment-its-riskier.html.

US Citizenship and Immigration Services. "H-1B Specialty Occupations, DOD Cooperative Research and Development Project Workers, and Fashion Models." Accessed 20 November 2020. https://www.uscis.gov/working-in-the-united-states/temporary-workers/h-1b-specialty-occupations-dod-cooperative-research-and-development-project-workers-and-fashion.

– "H-2A Temporary Agricultural Workers." Accessed 20 November 2020. https://www.uscis.gov/working-in-the-united-states/temporary-workers/h-2a-temporary-agricultural-workers.

Valiani, S. *Rethinking Unequal Exchange: The Global Integration of Nursing Labour Markets*. Toronto: University of Toronto Press, 2012.

Vernon, T. "Alberta Push to Suspend TFW Program Raising Concerns in Restaurant Industry." *Global News*, 30 June 2020. https://globalnews.ca/news/7126840/alberta-temporary-foreign-workers-kenney/.

Villegas, P.E. *North of El Norte: Illegalized Mexican Migrants in Canada*. Vancouver: UBC Press, 2020.

Vosko, L.F. "Legal but Deportable: Institutionalized Deportability and the Limits of Collective Bargaining among Participants in Canada's Seasonal Agricultural Workers Program." *Industrial and Labor Relations Review* 71, no. 4 (2018): 882–907.

Waldman, D.A., D. Wang, S.T. Hannah, B.P. Owens, and P.A. Balthazard. "Psychological and Neurological Predictors of Abusive Supervision." *Personnel Psychology* 71, no. 3 (2018): 399–421.

Wayne, J.H., R. Matthews, W. Crawford, and W.J. Casper. "Predictors and Processes of Satisfaction with Work-Family Balance: Examining the Role of Personal, Work, and Family Resources and Conflict and Enrichment." *Human Resource Management* 59, no. 1 (2000): 25–42.

Weikle, B. "COVID Outbreaks on Farms Reveal Crack in System that Migrant
    Workers Slip Through, Say Health-Care Workers." CBC Radio, *White
    Coat, Black Art*, 20 November 2020. https://www.cbc.ca/radio/whitecoat/
    covid-outbreaks-on-farms-reveal-crack-in-system-that-migrant-workers-slip-
    through-say-health-care-workers-1.5808489.
Wells, D., J. McLaughlin, A. Lyn, and A. Díaz Mendiburo. "Sustaining
    Precarious Transnational Families: The Significance of Remittances from
    Canada's Seasonal Agricultural Workers Program." *Just Labour: A Canadian
    Journal of Work and Society* 22 (2014): 144–67.
Wright, C.F., and A. Constantin. "Why Recruit Temporary Sponsored Skilled
    Migrants? A Human Capital Theory Analysis of Employer Motivations in
    Australia." *Australian Journal of Management* 46, no.1 (2021): 151–73.
Zhang, Y., and T.C. Bednall. "Antecedents of Abusive Supervision: A Meta-
    Analytic Review." *Journal of Business Ethics* 139 (2016): 455–71.
Zoeteweij-Turhan, M.H. "The Seasonal Workers Directive: '… but Some Are
    More Equal than Others.'" *European Labour Law Journal* 8, no. 1 (2017):
    28–44.

Index

hours, 95; respect and autonomy,
99; unpaid overtime, 94–5;
vulnerability to mistreatment of
TFWS, 17, 23, 102–3, 108
Canada Border Services Agency, 53
Canada Revenue Agency, 14, 105,
127
Canadian Chamber of Commerce,
135
Canadian Experience Class program,
103, 104
Canadian Federation for
Independent Business, 137
Canadian Horticultural Council, 8
Canadian immigration points
system, 89; policies, 89, 139, 156n4.
See also immigration consultants
Canadian Labour Board, 96, 122
Canadian Pension Plan, 12
caregivers. *See* in-home caregivers;
live-in caregivers
cashiers, 16, 52
Cedillo, L., 31, 33, 134
Certificat de sélection du Québec, 16
chef, 14, 31, 135, 152n31
Cheung, L., 27
China, 20, 36, 49, 92; Chinese
students, 43
College of Immigration and
Citizenship Consultants, 154n24
Comprehensive and Economic
Trade Agreement, 7
Comprehensive and Progressive
Agreement for Trans-Pacific
Partnership, 7
computer programmers, 38, 95
Constantine, A., 115
construction industry and workers,
20, 31, 72, 96
contract breaches, 36, 111
cooks, 40, 63, 93, 102, 113, 135

Costa Rica, 158n45
counter attendants, 38
Covid-19, 119, 145
Criminal Code of Canada, 154n27
Croatia, 20, 41, 103

deportation, 48; "deportability," 24,
27
differentiation-consolidation theory
(DCT), 98
domestic helpers, labourers, workers,
8, 9, 92, 93
Dominica, 10
Dubai, 95, 100

Eastern Caribbean countries, 8
Edmonton, 49, 114
El Salvador, 97
Emploi-Québec, 14
employers: and advertising jobs,
126; attitudes toward government
regulations, 126–9; comparisons
made by, 105–7; evaluation of
TFW program by, 109, 123–6;
hiring relatives, 81–3; home/
residence of, 12–13, 112; illegal
fees charged by, 30; and labour
availability, 119–22; and Labour
Market Impact Assessment (LMIA),
10–11; and LMIA application,
14–16; non-compliance of, 19, 109,
116–19, 132, 142, 143, 154n27; and
obligations to temporary foreign
workers (TFWS), 11–12; perspective
of, 6, 55–62, 127; prospective,
10, 14, 80, 98; "reluctant" and
"reckless," 19; and Seasonal
Agricultural Worker Program
(SAWP) workers, 11; and using
social networks, 80–1, 83. *See also*
managers

Temporary Foreign Worker (TFW)
program: compared with
International Mobility Program
(IMP), 7; diversity of, 9; evaluated
by employers as unreasonably
slow, 123–6; flaws of, 19; four
occupational streams of, 8;
overview of, 6–9; policies of
compared with international
ones, 88–108; recommended
modifications to, 134–46
*Temporary Foreign Worker Protection
Act* (2018) (British Columbia), 146
temporary foreign workers (TFWs):
closed work permits of, 43;
compared with IMP workers, 7;
cost-effectiveness of hiring, 115;
employers' obligations to, 11–12;
fear of retaliation of, 143; fewer
alternative employment options
of, 113; forging new ties in
Canada, 76–7; living conditions
of, 6; mistreatment of, 4–5, 19;
possible additional protections,
141–6; reduced social capital
of, 85; relations with Canadian
workers, 3–4; social isolation of,
26, 27, 73, 87; working in Seasonal
Agricultural Worker Program
(SAWP), 10. *See also* employers'
perceptions of TFW programs;
family members already in
Canada; family members brought
to Canada; family members left
behind; social capital
temporary foreign workers (TFWs)
and employment agencies
and immigration consultants:
differing goals of, 48–9; improved
regulation of, 65; information
asymmetries, 51–2, 62–4, 67–8;

remedies to problems, 64–7; and
risk, 53–5
Tham, J.-C., 32, 44
Tim Hortons, 30
Timor-Leste, 91
Tonga, 91
Toronto, 55, 56
tourism industry, 20, 57, 91, 99, 113,
120, 121, 125
training, 3, 12, 16, 24, 29, 41, 44, 47,
110, 111, 113, 120; safety training,
25, 38, 39, 95, 96
Trinidad and Tobago, 8, 10
truck drivers, 6, 16, 49, 73, 137
Tuvalu, 91

United Arab Emirates (UAE), 18, 88,
89, 93, 94, 108
United Kingdom, 89
United States, 7, 18, 89, 90, 98, 99,
107, 108, 138

Valiani, S., 30
Vanuatu, 91
verbal abuse, 28, 79, 20, 88,
videographers, 14, 41, 103, 152n32
Villegas, P., 48, 51
visas. *See* work visas
Vosko, L., 23

wages, 151n20, 152n25, 152n28,
152n31. *See also* high-wage
program; low-wage program;
median wages; minimum wage
wage theft, 17, 24, 30, 31, 116; illegal
employment fees, 25, 26, 30, 49,
116, 140
watchman, 93
West Indian Domestic Scheme, 8
work-life balance, 95; work–life
conflict, 87